Social Gardens

Social Gardens

Outdoor Spaces for Living and Entertaining

Charlotte M. Frieze

Photographs by Peter C. Jones

Stewart, Tabori & Chang
New York

Published in 1988 by
Stewart, Tabori & Chang, Inc.
740 Broadway, New York, New York 10003

Library of Congress Cataloging-in-Publication Data

Frieze, Charlotte M.
  Social gardens : outdoor spaces for living and entertaining /
Charlotte M. Frieze ; photographs by Peter C. Jones.
      p.   cm.

  ISBN 1-55670-047-4 : $40.00
    1. Gardens—United States—Design.   2. Gardens—United States—
Social aspects.   3. Gardens—United States—Design—Pictorial wo.
I. Title.
SB473.F835   1988
712′.6′0973—do19   88-15297
                                                              CIP

Distributed by Workman Publishing
708 Broadway, New York, New York 10003

Printed in Japan

10 9 8 7 6 5 4 3 2 1

Contents

The Intimate Garden

I remember a lovely tea in East Hampton. Under a clear blue, late-May sky, I was led through the garden to a secluded alcove beneath a stand of majestic pines. There, enclosed by a boxwood hedge and amidst a profusion of lilacs, a glorious table for four was set in pinks and lavenders, surrounded by cushioned wicker chairs. I savored the peacefulness as much as the wonderful array of delights: tea sandwiches of smoked salmon and watercress, warm scones served with Devonshire cream and strawberry preserves, elegant French pastries. As the branch-filtered sunlight warmed our table, we listened to the gentle rhythm of nearby ocean waves. Enclosed in a room with magic walls, we became intoxicated with pleasure.

Both personal and private, the intimate garden is a world unto itself. Safely tucked away in the niche of a hedge, or hidden at the end of an allée, intimate gardens are designed to accommodate just a few people, and are small paradises for relaxation, contemplation, and quiet conversation. They provide a relaxed ambience for small gatherings or a romantic setting for moonlit dinners. Although some may be large enough to accommodate an elaborate fish pond, others may simply contain a bench for two in the cool shelter of a grand, old blue Atlas cedar. Regardless, gardens of this variety should soothe the soul and refresh the eye.

Always self-contained, the character of any specific intimate garden evolves first from its enclosure, then from its focus. The enclosure can be used as a solid background to highlight the focus, such as a jet of water rising from a central pool. It can also establish an effective frame with which to direct the view. From gardens enclosed on all sides, to those that merely suggest enclosure, to gardens designed to incorporate elements from the surrounding landscape, the choice and combination of materials is limited only by the imagination: shrubs, trees, flowers, and vines; walls of brick, wood, or stone; pergolas and gazebos; waterfalls, fountains, and ponds; furniture and sculpture—all can have their place in an intimate garden.

Although the background is the important element in establishing the intimate garden, the key to success lies in the selection of the focus, since this will be what sets the tone and centers your attention. A gazebo, a

vine-covered pergola, or a fountain may beckon you into the garden, but it is the focus—what you see from inside the sitting area—that transports you to another world and completes the intimate experience. A white bench nestled among lilacs, dogwoods, and viburnums lures one along a narrow winding path to an intimate corner of a New England garden. Once seated on the bench, the focus shifts to the herbaceous border just visible through the trees. This garden, viewed through the many layers of moving branches, at once offers delight and privacy. It has become a favorite place for reading on a late spring afternoon when the shrubs are in bloom and the scent of lilies of the valley fills the air. Without having first seen the bench, however, one might never have taken the path and enjoyed the secrets revealed by this special garden.

Intimate gardens, conceived as garden rooms hidden from view, are often thought of as secret gardens—only the cognoscenti and the adventurous find them. A gate in an old garden wall or a lion standing guard might mark the entrance. By following narrow and circuitous paths that seem to lead nowhere, one will sometimes happen upon the private pleasure of a secret garden.

All elements of John Saladino's *giardino segreto* enhance its intimate qualities. Following the spiral set up by a series of paths

Pages 8–9: *This spectacular jet in Seattle, Washington* (left) *draws the visitor into a verdant setting beneath towering Douglas firs and provides the focus for a person seated on the stone bench. Its sounds contribute greatly to the both soothing and intriguing ambience.* Right: *Stones found miles away were put to good use as benches nestled harmoniously into the rhododendrons and astilbe in this Rhode Island woodland garden.*

Below: *A sculpture by George Rickey is both the centerpiece and focus from the traditional gazebo in a garden created within the foundation walls of an early nineteenth-century building in upstate New York.*

Opposite: *A collaboration of walls, fences, and hedges forms the enclosure essential for an intimate afternoon tea.*

The focus is crucial in establishing the tone of a garden: the classic draped figure (right) *is central to this formal Seattle garden whereas the sculpture of a young girl* (below) *sets the intimate mood in the garden of a Manhattan townhouse.*

and steps into this walled and hedged garden room in northwestern Connecticut, the visitor comes upon a high, surrounding hedge that permits a quick glimpse of the pool from which the garden radiates. Once inside, the pool becomes the garden's focus, a fragrant herbaceous border acting as a colorful foil to the pool's central jet fountain. The sound of the trickling water fills this intimate enclave as it focuses one's thoughts inward. A small window in the wall provides a counterpoint: a beautiful vista through the trees to the more open horseshoe garden beyond.

At Robin Hill in Norfolk, Connecticut, John Saladino has set an inviting late-afternoon picnic by the pool of his secret garden, where the guests will be soothed by the splashing of the jet and the sweet fragrance of the surrounding lilies.

WITHIN A VERDANT SHELTER

Both architectural and verdurous, pergolas and arbors act as points of transition in the garden while providing the experience of being inside a garden room. Vine-covered timbers overhead afford protection from the sun as well as privacy. Vertical supports define the sheltered space and, when softened by fragrant flowering vines, create an especially sensuous enclosure. As an architectural element, a pergola is often attached to the house and thus becomes a lovely shelter for outdoor dining or just conversation. In the garden, an arbor is usually freestanding, defining a space while also contributing a picturesque accent to the landscape.

In this garden, the owner's favorite place for reading is a bench surrounded by fragrant flowers and trees shimmering in the dappled Rhode Island sunlight.

The inclusion of climbing vines such as clematis serves not only to soften the hard edges of a stockade fence, but also to contribute a welcome touch of color.

Gardens are enhanced by the inclusion of special personal references. This sundial, passed from generation to generation, has contributed a spirit of family tradition to each successive garden it has graced.

Pergolas and arbors are as much focal points in the garden as tools with which to direct the view. When a bubbling fountain or an exquisite specimen tree is placed within the visual frame created by the structure, the eye is drawn into the adjacent garden. Placing such a focal point nearer the opening of the arbor obscures the view, thereby enclosing the space and enhancing the sense of intimacy. The use of either device enriches the experience of strolling or sitting in the dappled light of the arbor to one of private delight.

The pergola Richard Schadt designed for a couple in California's Marin County provides an elegant enclosure for a spa while adding a focus to the intimate garden adjacent to the master suite. Nestled into the hillside, this pergola provides privacy and contributes an airy, light feeling to the space. Bronze windbells designed by Paolo Soleri, suspended from the timbers above the spa, play an especially important role in establishing an environment conducive to relaxation. The rich sonorities of the windbells envelop the pergola, obscuring any suggestion of the outside world. Here is a place to unwind at the end of a long day: sitting back in the warm water, one can look up at the stars and let the day's tensions flow away.

In contrast, arbors call more attention to themselves. One vine-laden arbor is the

John Saladino added this circular pool to his secret garden at Robin Hill. Upon entering the garden, the niche in the distance continues to provide the central focus. When sitting within the niche, however, the focus shifts to the pool, subtly transforming one's perception of the space.

Below and opposite: A wisteria-laden arbor at Longwood Gardens in Delaware creates an intimate outdoor room in which to sit and enjoy the play of light through the arbor's structure and the intertwining vines and brilliant blossoms it hosts.

centerpiece of an expansive, informal flower garden in East Hampton. Here, the waves of flowers bedecking the arbor were chosen to provide continuous bloom. From the first fragrant white blossoms of wisteria in spring to the trumpet vine and clematis in summer, the arbor flows gracefully into the surrounding sea of brilliant-colored wildflowers.

As a colorful frame to the view, an arbor can also create a visually exciting moment in the garden. Within an arbor laden with heavy, lavender wisteria blossoms in Delaware, the focus of brilliant fuchsia azaleas set dramatically against a deep blue sky offers a rich and intriguing kaleidoscope of colors.

Trees provide their own intimate setting within the shelter of their branches. Walking through an allée of pleached silver lindens in Newport, Rhode Island one is embraced by the branches. Like an arbor, the branches subtly define the space while focusing the view on the garden in the distance. Their enclosure acts as an intimate transition between the large, open lawns and the meticulously designed, formal planting beds that comprise the gardens of the estate. A small grove of honey locust trees, heavily pruned to form a feathery ceiling, also provides intimate shelter in the garden. A picnic in the dappled shade, with leaves gently rustling above, can be at once soothing and refreshing.

At Winterthur, a former DuPont estate in Delaware, the wide-spreading branches of an ancient blue Atlas cedar provide an intimate enclosure for this traditional teak bench.

The pergola encompassing this Marin County spa is also invitingly open to the warming sun or the glistening stars.

GAZEBOS: GARDEN HOUSES OF THE IMAGINATION

Originally designed as small, open buildings with solid roofs from which to "gaze out" at the garden, gazebos are now often enclosed by full or half walls with large openings to direct the view. Like pavilions or small summerhouses, they are more substantial architectural garden elements than pergolas or arbors. Enclosed and private, a gazebo provides an intimate place for relaxation, which is at once in the garden and separate from it. Whether constructed of rustic wood or intricate ironwork, or perhaps painted white with classical detailing, gazebos are picturesque garden structures intended purely for pleasure.

Richard Anderson conceived of his gazebo as a rustic shelter to "provide a cool, refreshing, and private place to sit, to read, or to do nothing at all." Anderson has created a large, magical garden that combines open lawn with intimate spaces set apart by lush borders with perennials, ferns, and groundcovers. Upon entering the garden, one's initial response is of wonderment that such a verdant, countrylike space could exist hidden behind six townhouses in downtown Albany.

Below and opposite: *Architectural elements like gazebos provide garden hideaways in which to relax at the same time that they set the tone. This picturesque, rustic shelter* (left) *summons up images of the Adirondacks but it is actually tucked into a countrylike space that was created behind six townhouses in downtown Albany, New York. From its cool embrace, the view of a lush, natural setting assists enormously in the banishment of the vestiges of urban life.*

Exotic, wrought iron tassel fringe found during an expedition to a favorite junkyard adds the finishing touches to this gazebo on Shelter Island. Surrounded by a sea of "Betty Prior" pink roses, it becomes a fantasy worthy of the Arabian Nights.

Anderson's gazebo is nestled amidst a rich tapestry woven of the textures and colors contributed by such plantings as rudbeckia, peonies, daylilies, feathery ostrich ferns, and blue spruce, all arranged against a backdrop of large Norway maples. With the creative combination of woodland plants and perennials most often associated with formal herbaceous borders, this lush corner of the garden enhances the garden's fanciful quality. From within the enclosure of the gazebo, one's view is directed through evergreen trees, thereby creating the illusion of being in a large natural setting. This touch of the Adirondacks in the middle of Albany is so unexpected that it transports the visitor from the city to the mountains.

Yet a gazebo might as easily transport one to another, imaginary world. Lisa Stamm and Dale Booher's gazebo in Shelter Island does just that. Designed and built by Dale, this gazebo is a fantasy right out of the *Arabian Nights*: exotic wrought iron tassel fringe hangs from the eaves; translucent white curtains wave in the breeze; in the cool shade, inviting white overstuffed cushions await. From the shelter of the gazebo one witnesses the sparks set off by the vibrant pinks of Lisa's rose garden as they contrast with the brilliant blue swimming pool.

A Post Modern gazebo in the hills above Los Angeles provides a cool retreat from the hot California sun. Set against the high retaining walls, the gazebo acts as a powerful foreground element, fostering an illusion of distance within the confines of the steep canyon slopes.

The owners of this Rhode Island gazebo enjoy dining here as they watch the play of the evening sunlight on their adjacent garden.

Harmony in the Garden

Sound is fundamental in creating an intimate atmosphere. As hedges, fences, and other garden structures establish a visual intimacy, sound—or the elimination of intrusive noise—is essential to sustaining the experience. Giving thoughtful consideration to existing noise conditions, one can design the garden either to add or subtract sound. Heedless of hedges and walls, the noise of traffic and other nearby activities can destroy the planned peaceful atmosphere. By including compensating sound (whether natural or manmade) in the overall design, intrusive noise can be masked successfully. The gentle rustling of leaves or the soft cooing of doves, the splashing of water as it falls from one pool to another, windchimes and bells—all enhance the garden experience while warding off the intrusion of the outside world.

In the city it is especially important to include sound in a garden design. By distracting guests from the noise of nearby traffic one sets the scene for them to relax and more thoroughly enjoy the pleasures of the garden. Entertaining on a city terrace is enhanced by the addition of windchimes or the sounds of water flowing over rocks and splashing into a pool at the terminus of a waterfall.

The residents of this dovecote are a constant delight as they flutter among the trees, splash in the birdbaths, and swathe the terrace in the sound of their gentle cooing.

In designing a walled outdoor room for a hot tub adjacent to a swimming pool, Alice Pickman selected plant materials that would both visually and sonically enhance the experience of relaxation. Inspired by Japanese courtyard gardens, Pickman planted golden bamboo and Japanese maples, which spill over the wall surrounding the hot tub. The rustling of the leaves establishes an ambience of tranquility that transports the mind from the rural Massachusetts landscape to the serenity of the Far East.

Birds often contribute the element that completes the desired ambience in an intimate garden. They are a delight both with their songs and their activity. Diane McGuire, a Boston landscape architect who takes into consideration "all experiences in the garden—both visual and auditory," often includes flowering-plant materials such as *Filipendula* and *Monarda* to attract hummingbirds to intimate sitting areas. For the same reason—as well as the fact that they provide privacy—another garden designer, in Piedmont, California, has incorporated citrus trees in the plans for a deck.

Whereas hummingbirds are attracted to the nectar of flowers, songbirds are attracted to gardens by plant materials selected for their fruit and twigs, as well as

Opposite and below: *With their songs and activity, birds often complete an intimate setting. Birdbaths, houses, and feeders can be ornamental as well as functional, and when well placed, can serve as centerpieces for elegant plantings.*

Overleaf: *Dining within the embrace of towering beech trees filled with the owner's family of white doves is always a special experience. A birdbath, nestled in the hosta and euonymous next to the terrace, often tempts the doves down from the treetops bringing their beauty right to the table.*

Opposite: *A thatch-roofed birdfeeder adds a touch of the English countryside to a garden near Newport, Rhode Island.*

Stylized, natural, traditional—birdbaths come in all shapes and designs. The birdbath at top was sculpted by Lloyd Lawton from a stone found near its present site.

their flowers. An arbor in Connecticut was sited in the middle of a meadow of wildflowers where cosmos, cornflowers, black-eyed Susans, and asters attract an array of colorful songbirds. Their songs drift into the intimate enclosure of the arbor as they swoop and flutter above the meadow. In New Jersey, a natural planting of shrubs and small trees entices songbirds to frequent a small fish pool in a woodland garden. The birds are attracted by the aromatic twigs of spicebush and the berries of red-osier dogwood, highbush-cranberry, and juneberries as well as a variety of hollies. The resulting chirping of the many small birds lends a special, personal scale to a bench otherwise dwarfed by a canopy of mature maples and oaks.

Feeders, baths, and houses for birds are attractive garden ornaments that ensure a continual flurry of birds in the garden. A multistoried dovecote is an elegant addition to a Rhode Island terrace. The doves fly freely throughout the intimate dining area nestled beneath majestic copper beech trees, always returning to their roost. Above the rustling of the leaves, their fluttering wings and cooing fill the garden with romance, heightening an already pleasureful experience.

Silhouetted against skimmia, rhododendrons, and azaleas, an antique birdbath becomes an elegant focal point at the terminus of a Seattle garden path.

Opposite: Birds, butterflies, and bees are all welcomed into this Norfolk, Connecticut garden.

Overleaf: Richard Anderson believes that every successful garden must include water; for his Albany, New York garden the solution is a half-barrel bearing water hyacinths and goldfish (left).
In a Rhode Island garden (right), a prefabricated pool was the answer. Here natural stone, a waterfall, and carefully chosen plantings all work together to obscure the otherwise regular edges.

WEAVING TEXTURE INTO THE GARDEN

The textures of the plant materials included in a garden room contribute to the sensual experience of that space. The approach to John Saladino's *giardino segreto* is carpeted with moss that stimulates the senses, both with its soft and luxuriant texture, and by its brilliant hues as it is highlighted by shafts of light filtering down through the branches of towering evergreen trees. In California's Napa Valley, Jack Chandler has incorporated massive clumps of an ornamental grass, *Pennisetum ruppelii*, in the design of the terrace adjacent to his swimming pool and spa. Their graceful, delicate pink inflorescences soften the hard stone surfaces and establish an inviting, relaxing environment.

With the imaginative use of texture, a garden enclosed by walls of evergreens is a year-round delight. The glossy surfaces of magnolia and boxwood leaves contrast dramatically with the leathery leaves of rhododendrons in a Washington, D.C. garden. In the summer, the lacy texture of Japanese maple leaves is elegantly combined with the waving plumes of ornamental grasses and the bright-yellow petals of rudbeckia. Near Newport, Rhode Island, imaginatively massed shrubs, grasses, and peren-

The blades of ornamental grasses, colorful flowering perennials, and the glossy leaves of boxwood and rhododendron are skillfully interwoven in this Washington, D.C. garden.

This regal lion acts as sentry as he lies contentedly before the sensuous moss and rustic fencing bounding the path to John Saladino's secret garden in Norfolk, Connecticut.

Overleaf: *Since it is such a challenge to grow outside its native Chile, this climbing perennial* (left), *the Flameflower* (Tropaeolium speciosum), *is the pride of Lakewold in Tacoma, Washington. The statue of a scholar* (right), *swathed in a sensuous tapestry of vines, shrubs, and perennials, has stood guard over this small pool at Lakewold since it was brought from Japan in the 1920s.*

nials form the walls for a series of interconnecting outdoor rooms. In one such area, bamboo and feathery ornamental grasses accentuate the strong, seemingly inflexible, lines of the rhododendrons, while the corridor leading to another is formed by parallel rows of *Cryptomeria japonica*. Throughout this garden the many patterns and textures of the leaves are interwoven to surround the rooms in magical tapestries of greens. These garden rooms, carpeted with velvety lawns and sculpted from masses of rhododendrons, are a refreshing retreat on a hot July day.

The size and shape of leaves blend to make up the garden's texture. In this Rhode Island garden, the fine texture of a weeping hemlock contrasts wonderfully with the bamboo, Arundinaria viridistriata, *and the large, round leaves of* Petasides japonica.

A boardwalk leads the way through an allée of Cryptomeria japonica "Lobii."

Sculptor Marge Hammond created this bench in a Portland, Oregon garden. Set to the side of a raked-gravel path, it nestles amidst native Gaultheria, which the Indians called Salal.

Opposite: *A rock garden tumbles over the hillside, unfolding beneath this sheltered terrace, which also has a spectacular view of the rugged New England coast.*

The experience of climbing this stone staircase in Portland, Oregon becomes a beautiful adventure as one wanders by the textural planting of miniature roses, ferns, sedums, and a multitude of perennials. Awaiting the climber is the lawn terrace above.

For years, the owner of this Seattle garden believed she had the only fall-blooming crocus in the state of Washington. One heartbreaking day, a horticulturalist informed her that they were actually Colchicum, a member of the lily family. She now calls them the "bogus crocus."

The evening sunlight confers its deep, rich hues on this lovely Portland, Oregon landscape, accentuating its already sensuous tactility.

PERFUME ON THE WIND

Fragrance completes the experience of the intimate garden. The scent of lilacs in the breeze on a late-spring evening can draw guests into a secret garden. Surrounding a pool and spa in California, the sweet aromas from lemon and orange trees, followed by those of star jasmine, sweet olive, and honeysuckle, fill the air with romance from early spring through the fall. Relaxing in the spa, one becomes intoxicated by the fragrance of the blossoms.

Although fragrance is most often associated with flowers, in many plants it is the leaves that contain the aromatic essences. The leaves of wintergreen, mint, and thyme must be crushed to release their scent, for example. A dining terrace in New England was designed to take full advantage of this characteristic, its fieldstones having been interplanted with thyme and lavender. When crossing the terrace, each step unleashes delicious fragrances, and the dining table is swathed in a rich, wonderful perfume.

An exquisite garden in Seattle was conceived by Tim Holtschlag to appeal to all the senses. A wonderfully intimate space hidden behind a finely crafted gate of bam-

The sweet fragrance of pink lavender mingles with the sea breeze, enveloping all who sit upon this inviting teak bench.

boo, it embraces the spirit of a Japanese garden and encourages contemplation while incorporating the element of surprise. The masterful use of fragrance, focus, texture, and sound delights the soul as well as the eye. Passing through its threshold, the visitor is transported into another dimension of pleasure. The lush green foliage enwrapping the garden allows complete surrender to the peace and tranquility of this private paradise. One's thoughts are set free to meander through the many levels of this extraordinary garden.

Inspired by the drama of the Cascade Mountains, where he often goes to relax, Holtschlag created this garden for Gary Nacci in which friends can experience the sense of freedom felt in the mountains at the same time as they enjoy the intimacy of enclosure. He has achieved this by incorporating Japanese techniques of illusion. Straight, tall trunks of firs and dogwoods, pruned to a six-foot height, rise majestically from a delicate carpet of mosses and ferns. They appear much larger than they are and pull forward visually as their green tones contrast with the dark-green background of rhododendrons. From the bench by the gate, a Japanese lantern carved by Nacci is close to eye level, filling a large area of focus. The garden unfolding in the distance seems much farther away.

Utilizing contrasting leaf textures and Japanese-inspired techniques of illusion, this garden in Seattle brings to mind Washington State's monumental Cascade Mountains, even though it lies within the confines of a small backyard. The path shown meanders through carpets of moss as well as Corsican mint which, when stepped upon, releases a wonderful fragrance.

Opposite: *Handcarved by its owner, this stone lantern marking the entrance to a Seattle garden sets a contemplative tone. When lit, candles hidden inside cast a gentle glow on summer evenings.*

For evenings with friends, Nacci bathes the garden in the soft, warm glow of candles placed in the lanterns. The nearby ferns, mosses, and shrubs are gently highlighted, while the firs at the boundary disappear into the darkness, casting the garden into a realm both endless and magical.

Following a stone path as it winds around the house and past a pond through Irish moss and Corsican mint, all the senses are stimulated by the sequence of garden experiences. As the view of the garden opens up to include a series of miniature waterfalls and pools, the gentle murmur of water descending between the rocks fills the air. Beginning as a thin cascade hidden within the dense growth of rhododendrons and azaleas, the water flow expands into a larger waterfall before ending in a lovely woodland pond. The variety of sounds occasioned by these falls blends beautifully with that of water flowing from a nearby chute into a lily pond. Throughout the garden, attention is focused by the sounds of water splashing and trickling, further separating the garden from the outside world and enhancing its special intimacy.

This lovely, old climbing rose stimulates all the senses as it greets visitors to an enclosed seaside garden in Rhode Island.

Chapter 2

Entrances

The entrance to a house is the scene for the beginning of every social experience and is therefore instrumental in setting the tone for all occasions. The treatment of the entry drive, front walk, and doorway contributes significantly to defining the personality of a house and thus establishes a strong framework for the relationship between indoor and outdoor entertaining spaces.

As in an intimate garden, focus, scale, texture, fragrance, and sound are integral to entrance design. With these elements one can draw attention to the house while establishing a style that is continued throughout the garden. For example, a house in a wooded landscape presents an image of being in harmony with its setting—as well as one of permanence—as lichen-covered boulders and the woods come right up to its front-entrance terrace. In a more populated area, a high gate or wall can enclose the house, setting it apart from others. A grey-shingled cottage in Rhode Island is accentuated by an expansive lawn bordered by a stone wall covered with a sea of pink roses that date back over one hundred years. Upon rounding the corner and catching a first glimpse of the house, the roses provide an immediate identity and bid one welcome.

THE ENTRANCE DRIVE: INTIMATIONS OF THINGS TO COME   As the transition between public and private spaces, the entrance drive introduces and establishes the tone of the social experience. Stone pillars, a fence, gate, or specimen tree are all useful in assisting guests in identifying the entrance. The line of approach, however, is the most critical element in determining the character of a property. Because the approach must be designed to accommodate such automobile requirements as turning radii, grading, and parking, it influences both the location of the house on its site and the arrangement of all its outdoor spaces.

The surface of the drive is also important and should be in harmony with the setting and the style of the house. A curving, unpaved drive is in keeping with a country locale while a gravel drive can be either informal or formal. Fine grey gravel edged with granite pavers, or red gravel edged with brick, provide clean, formal approaches, while multicolored, coarse crushed stone is more fitting for a farm. Asphalt, the most common driveway surface, requires little maintenance and wears well. Whatever the surface, it is important the driveway be well maintained and lend a favorable impression. This is both the beginning of the social experience and the end. An entrance drive in need of repair can leave one shaken and exhausted from the effort of avoiding potholes. No matter how enjoyable the occasion, thoughts of the obstacle course awaiting upon departure will lurk in the back of the visitor's mind during a party, and linger on as an unpleasant memory later.

The progression from street to house is enhanced by careful planning of the drive in conjunction with the plantings. Masses of evergreen and deciduous shrubs planted along a winding drive add year-round visual interest. By obstructing the view of the house along this curving approach, these plant massings heighten the anticipation of what is to come while offering privacy from the road. A drive sweeping gracefully in front of a house is much more dramatic than one stopping abruptly at garage doors.

A straight entrance drive leads one directly to the destination. As the house is always within view, the addition of a visual frame or partial screen heightens the experience of approach. In New England, parallel rows of grand old maple trees add majesty to the straight entrance drive at

These lovely roses have marked the entrance to a home near Newport, Rhode Island for over a hundred years.

Yellow Gate Farm. Passing through the gates, one enters a dappled tunnel created by the canopy of conjoining tree branches, while the repetition of trunks forms a continuous frame for the farmhouse. The combined effect of the long, straight driveway reinforced by rows of maple trees is mesmerizing: one feels irresistibly drawn toward the destination.

As at Yellow Gate Farm, the garden experience of a guest at Robin Hill, John Saladino's Connecticut home, begins at the gate. Here, the visitor leaves the country road and enters a woodland park of small-blossom azaleas. The plantings seem to become less wild and more formal as one progresses up the winding drive toward the house. The fields of azaleas gradually segue into woods of rhododendrons, mountain laurel, hemlocks, and maples edged by pachysandra, luxuriant ferns, and small areas of lawn, creating a mood of enchantment. At the house, the drive terminates in a bright, formal courtyard enclosed by whitewashed brick walls covered with climbing hydrangeas and edged with beds of vinca. This walled courtyard effectively couples the entrance drive with the Palladian brick house, establishing a gracious space for the host to greet his guests.

In the Pacific Northwest, the awesome scale of the native primeval landscape helps to establish the character of the approach to a magnificent château-style house in Seat-

A splash of color at an entrance attracts attention and always bids a welcome to guests. Clockwise from top left: *An herbaceous border and roses greet visitors to a Rhode Island home, while a flowering crabapple and a bright-red door identify the front entrance to a home in East*

Hampton. At two other homes near Newport, Rhode Island, greeting is extended by means of a wall smothered in honeysuckle and roses, which distinguishes the entry drive, or an arbor—covered with trumpet vine that marks the transition between gardens.

tle's Highlands. Utilizing the landscape as it winds its way through clusters of two-hundred-foot-high indigenous firs, the owners have managed to direct the arriving visitor's focus to the house, glowing in the soft sunlight that filters through the evergreen trees. At a distance, the house appears dwarfed by the great height of the firs. However, as the driveway emerges from the forest and sweeps in front of the house, a great shift in scale is experienced. Suddenly, the house becomes more impressive as it fills the view completely. The culmination of the approach lies in the house itself, an elegant structure whose design is in harmony with its setting.

THE FRONT WALK: DOWN A GARDEN PATH

Arriving at a party and not knowing which doorbell to ring, or having a fresh tear in one's stockings courtesy of a thorny shrub can be very disconcerting and can start an evening off on a sour note. Like the transition from the driveway to the front door, the front walk plays a leading role in welcoming a guest. The walk must be easily identifiable, its paving surface solid and even. The goal is to lead the visitor effortlessly to the front door. But, while a walk's primary purpose is navigational,

Colorful perennials welcome visitors to these Rhode Island homes (top), *while classical gates* (bottom) *invite one to step into gardens in Westport, Connecticut* (left), *and Winterthur* (right).

Overleaf: *With its tunnel of conjoining maples, the entrance drive to Yellow Gate Farm draws the arriving visitor toward the house. In spring and summer the canopy is a rich green, while in autumn it is ablaze with yellows and oranges. The repeating trunks and interlacing branches frame the house in winter.*

creating a garden around it can enhance the experience of entrance, as the fragrances of scented flowers and herbs blend with the rich colors and textures of flowering shrubs, perennials, and ornamental grasses to stimulate and thrill all the senses.

A front walk planted for all seasons is distinguished by its array of color and is a joy to follow. For a home in the Georgetown district of Washington, D.C., landscape architects Oehme, van Sweden and Associates designed a gently curving brick path that, with assistance from a profusion of perennials and grasses, directs guests to a small entry terrace adjacent to the front door. Just large enough to accommodate a teak bench for two, this terrace both provides an additional focus for the walk and offers a comfortable place from which to view the garden.

Shrubs and trees reinforce the line of a front walk in Rhode Island, establishing its identity. A variety of evergreen trees and shrubs were chosen for color as well as texture to create an entrance that is visually exciting and, most of all, fun. Walking up the fieldstone path through the hedge of *Arborvitae plicatum*, past a beautiful specimen blue Atlas cedar, then up the stone stairway marked by a pair of carefully trained and pruned junipers, one is intrigued while being directed by the imaginative use of shrubs. The front door is identified by an impressive espaliered

Below: *Walled entrance courtyards such as the one at Robin Hill, John Saladino's Norfolk, Connecticut home, establish a gracious space in which to greet one's guests.*

Opposite: *When seeking to provide definition and enclosure—and when trying to demarcate the passing from one garden space into another—gates are an excellent solution. Here, the gate marks the entrance to a glorious, walled perennial garden in Westport, Connecticut.*

Korean dogwood just visible through the trees at the end of the path. During June, its white starlike blossoms are in brilliant contrast to the dark siding of the house and the evergreen shrubs.

Site conditions often prevent architects from locating the front door where it would be most visible. The circulation system must therefore take on the responsibility of clearly leading guests to the threshold. A change in paving patterns—such as from a gravel drive to a brick path, or from granite pavers to a bluestone walk—can identify a front path; low hedges and specimen trees can then be put to use as accents for the entrance. In Portland, Oregon, where steep slopes often dictate the siting of a home, Barbara Fealy utilized a rock retaining wall to direct visitors to the front door. At the driveway, guests enter a wide path of warm, brown Oregon stone, which fits smoothly into the gentle curve of the retaining wall. Reinforcing the approach is a planting of white azaleas and pink rhododendrons beneath a pair of *Styrax japonica* on the other side of the walk, next to the house. The great mass of the wall is softened with a planting of heathers, heaths, ferns, and yew, all of which collaborate to create a natural transition from the surrounding woods to the house. The path is clear, and in all seasons one feels instantly welcome.

Scale is integral to all garden design. Here native Western red cedars and Douglas firs tower two hundred feet above the entrance drive, elegantly framing yet dwarfing this substantial château-style home in the Seattle Highlands. As one nears the house, the driveway emerges from the woods and one's perception of scale shifts completely as the house fills the view.

Planted with a colorful array of perennials and ornamental grasses, this herringbone-pattern brick walk in Georgetown entices the visitor to follow it any time of year.

Gardens are perhaps most wonderful when designed as landscapes to be explored. An entrance path that continues around the house to the outdoor living area provides the opportunity for visitors to be led through a series of uninterrupted garden experiences. Guests remember with great pleasure the discovery of an extraordinary hidden vista that burst into view as a garden path brought them around a corner. At Dutch Strawbridge's Rhode Island home, for example, the path *is* the garden. In July, the walk, ablaze with brilliant yellow sedum, directs the visitor around the house to the privacy of the rose garden, then to the pool beyond. First drawn through a dark shrubbery tunnel, the visitor is then greeted by the brilliant sunlight of the backyard. While venturing on toward the pergola-shaded deck and pool, the visitor is caressed by a breeze filled with the delicious fragrance of the multitude of roses.

Like the Strawbridge garden, a path in Portland, Oregon permits entrance to the garden without necessitating walking through the house. Here, the tall, white garden gate becomes "the front door." The stepping-stone path leads first to a lush, open "foyer" framed by evergreen shrubs with accents of colorful annuals. As guests continue along the path, a pergola heavily laden with wisteria enfolds them, making them feel welcome. Like the tunnel of

Opposite: *This handsome cast-stone lion guards the entrance to a Rhode Island home.*

Below: *A topiary yew is a wonderfully amusing punctuation for the front entrance to this Rhode Island home.*

shrubbery in the Strawbridge garden, this pergola is just long enough to heighten anticipation when one approaches the deck that overlooks the Willamette River.

THE ENTRANCE TERRACE: AN INVITING COURTYARD

For some, the forecourt, or entrance terrace, is not only a place to greet guests, it is one in which actually to entertain. Large enough to accommodate several people comfortably, an entry terrace is most successful when enclosed by a wall, fence, or hedge, and when partially covered to provide protection from the elements outside the front door.

Such an entrance provides a gracious welcome to a home in coastal New England. Perched on a hill, ten feet above the driveway, the front entrance is obscured from view. Hideo Sasaki, with the assistance of Lloyd Lawton, added a formal forecourt at the top of a wide, inviting staircase, thereby calling attention to the entrance and establishing an ambience of welcome. Upon opening the gate to this courtyard garden, guests enter a peaceful, very private room with a carpet of brilliant yellow sedum and a ceiling of red pine; the sounds of the trickling fountain and birds chattering in the trees is immediately soothing. An adjacent covered terrace is a

Below: *Site conditions often dictate the location of the front door. Here, for example, landscape architect Barbara Fealy has utilized wide stone steps and a rock retaining wall planted with ferns, yew, and heath to direct the visitor to a hidden entrance in Portland, Oregon.*

favorite place for summer entertaining, and from the terrace the garden becomes a lovely focus for a party.

Japanese sensibilities are also integral to the experience of entry to a home in the Santa Barbara hills. Landscape architect Isabelle C. Greene meticulously selected stones for their iridescence in order to approximate closely the flow of water. Beginning in the forecourt, they form a path that is the thread that ties a series of gardens together. Upon entering the white-walled forecourt, the visitor is immediately impressed by its Zen-like qualities. By using a variety of drought-resistant plant materials combined with many textures of stone, Greene has created a space with great intrinsic harmony that both relaxes and intrigues. A pool, inspired by the owner's memories of the High Sierra, is a refreshing accent in this arid landscape. Drawn to the pool by the aquatic plants and the gentle intermittent bubbles, rising as though from a spring, guests catch a first glimpse of the path originating at the pool's edge. The sparkling, streamlike path entices one from the forecourt's cool shade around the corner of the house, between carefully placed boulders planted with succulents, to the living room terrace with its spectacular view toward the sea. Enclosed by a stark, white wall topped with a delicate stroke of fuchsia bougainvillaea, the south-facing terrace shimmers

This path is the garden. Visitors are drawn along its course, which is ablaze with yellow sedum, through a shrubbery tunnel to the rose garden and pool beyond.

in the brilliant California sunlight. Here the stream of stones seems to disappear briefly, only to surface again in the series of terraced gardens below.

On hillside sites it is often impossible to construct terraces of brick or flagstone. In such cases, decks connected by stairs direct movement from the road to the front door. When a California couple renovated their Marin County home, one of their primary goals was to create as much space for outdoor entertaining as possible within the constraints of their hillside site. To increase the outdoor living area, landscape architect Richard Schadt eliminated the driveway and moved the garage to the street above the house. He then designed a series of decks and terraces that begins at the street, integrating all parts of the house with the garden as it traverses the steep hillside to the swimming pool on the lowest level. A shingled gateway identifies the entry walk that leads down the hillside to the forty-foot-long entrance deck.

Nestled beneath the overhanging branches of an evergreen, native oak, with a spectacular view across the top of eucalyptus trees, this entrance deck beckons and welcomes. An Indian totem marks the recessed entry and flowering plants add bright contrast to the warm brown of the shingled enclosing walls. Two pairs of floor-to-ceiling glass doors, opening out

Opposite: *For this Portland, Oregon condominium, Barbara Fealy designed a garden path, a useful device for permitting entrance to the back deck without necessitating a trip through the house.*

Below: *A front-entrance terrace provides a gracious welcome to visitors arriving at this home on the New England coast.*

onto the deck, permit a relaxed flow from the living room. Furnished with a heavy wooden table and chairs, the deck has become an extension of the house and a favorite place to serve a casual Sunday brunch.

The car may have been banished from this Marin County garden, but in one Portland, Oregon garden, the car has become an integral part. In fact, landscape architect Barbara Fealy has introduced these clients to the concept of the "drive-in party," and has designed the perfect setting. After first enjoying a lovely drive through woods of massive, native fir trees, then entering the gates close to the house, guests are surprised to find themselves driving almost into the center of the party—for the driveway leads directly up to the front door, which is opposite the entrance to the terrace. The drive then loops around the terrace and back to the entry gates.

This entrance terrace is distinguished from the aggregate driveway by its contrasting surface of brown Oregon stone, and was designed with three separate entertaining areas for dining and living. A gracefully curving stairway leads from the terrace to the upper section of the driveway where it widens into a terrace large enough to accommodate a band. A retaining wall, just the right height for sitting, swoops around the terrace, forming pleasant recessed areas. While the terrace is large enough to accommodate a sit-down din-

For sites with steep slopes, decks are often more suitable than terraces. This large entrance deck in Marin County, California has become a favorite place for the owners to entertain.

ner-dance for one hundred, the alcoves are warm and intimate, perfect for a luncheon with a few friends. This couple's parties are especially vibrant in spring when the surrounding shrub border is ablaze with azaleas, rhododendrons, and viburnums.

When another Portland couple renovated their house, integration with the garden was a primary goal. Here Fealy designed a large outdoor living area that includes two new terraces, an elegant swimming pool and, most important, a new, impressive entrance. The addition of a brick wall and a wide entrance terrace distinguishes their home from that of their neighbors. The circulation system ties it all together: a gravel path leads guests from the terrace at the front door through a wrought iron gate into the surrounding garden. With gracefully sweeping curves, it guides guests effortlessly through a beautifully maintained apple orchard before opening up onto the first of a series of terraces used for dining and entertaining. Along the path are "resting" areas where one can curl up with a book and a cup of coffee.

Space limitations are among the greatest influences on the design of entrance terraces. In the case of the new entrance to the Pacific Palisades home of Elsa and Peter Myers, the house was built into a steep hillside, the street barely a car-length away. Here, a retaining wall was as much a neces-

In the environmentally sensitive landscape of the Santa Barbara Hills, water is always a primary design consideration. Here, Isabelle C. Greene has used a palette of drought-resistent plant materials, along with stones of varying texture, to create a path that has an ambience of contemplative quiet as it leads to the outdoor entertaining area.

sity as a design element. By adding a gate to the opening between the house and the high, white retaining wall, landscape architects Emmet L. Wemple & Associates defined and enclosed the entrance area, creating a private courtyard in which the Myerses can greet their guests. A fountain opposite the front door masks the sound of passing cars while providing a focus for the space. This new plan is sensitive to the original design by Cliff May and it also ensures privacy and a comfortable approach to the outdoor living areas.

The Myerses enjoy entertaining on the terrace and deck, both of which offer dramatic views of the city and the ocean beyond. The flagstone walk in warm earth tones, flanked by the house on one side and the retaining wall on the other, is like a narrow hallway leading guests from the front entry to the outdoor living room. The deep, overhanging roof creates great drama as its casts sharp shadows on the stark, white walls. At night, light reflecting off the walls casts a gentle glow over the pool and terrace. Terra cotta pots filled with sculptural succulents and brilliant annuals provide accents of color throughout the entry.

As do the best examples of entrance design, this courtyard and walk immediately intrigue and entice the visitor. The courtyard enfolds, while also enhancing the style of the house. Most of all, the entrance makes one feel welcome.

Sharp shadows created by the brilliant California sunlight enrich the brief journey from the entrance courtyard to the outdoor entertaining areas of this sensitively renovated Pacific Palisades house, originally designed by Cliff May.

Circulation systems tie the various aspects of a property together. In Portland, Oregon, this sweeping gravel path leads visitors from the front-entrance terrace, beneath a canopy of apple-tree branches, to the back garden and pool.

Chapter 3

The Backyard

There once was a time, not so long ago, when people sat out in their front yards, catching up with friends or simply watching the world go by. But when horses were replaced by Fords, they retreated to the backyard, away from all the dirt and noise of passing automobiles. Today, the backyard is the place to relax and entertain.

Backyard gardens come in all sizes. While they often can be tiny, many are of sufficient scope to include living and dining areas as well as outdoor kitchens; even larger gardens can include pools, spas, lawns, and play areas. Regardless of size, however, the most successful are both visually exciting and refreshing to experience.

In Los Angeles, where backyards are lush throughout the year, the goal is to create a garden that looks cool and is refreshing even when the thermometer reaches the 100° mark. Pamela Burton and Katie Spitz have achieved this in a garden they designed for a noted film director who wanted a space in which he could entertain as well as work. Burton and Spitz drew upon English gardens for their inspiration. A profusion of perennials and annuals spills over the edge of the freeform swimming pool. Violets provide the groundcover in a shady spot that is punctuated with the spikes of daylilies, irises, and ferns, all conspiring to convey a refreshingly wild and mysterious mood. Low mounds of pink impatiens and sweet alyssum growing between the stones in the path introduce the garden color right at the terrace steps and, as these colorful interruptions in the path continue on, they draw guests further and further into the garden.

Burton and Spitz used the sharp, bright California sunlight to shape the perceived space. As seen from both the interior and exterior entertaining spaces, evergreen trees that were carefully positioned at the edge of the property provide a solid ground against which the brilliant yellows and pinks of the herbaceous border glow. Atop the encompassing ivy-covered wall bougainvillaea steps forward from the dark-green backdrop of ivy

leaves. This play of contrasting colors along with light and shade lends to the relaxed and refreshing ambience, increasing the perception of depth while unifying the garden.

THE OUTDOOR ROOM—WITH ITS VIEW

To design the backyard garden, begin by determining its focal point and its function. Whether an intimate garden room hidden at a distance from the house or a terrace acting as an extension of the indoor entertaining areas, the garden should draw people into its embrace. Strong visual links between house and garden, such as those established by the use of French doors and large windows, are helpful in inviting guests out into the garden, especially when such apertures frame exquisite views.

When Diane McGuire agreed to landscape the ten-acre property of a contemporary house along the New England coast, she began by assessing the potential vistas. Since this new house was designed to include an entire side of glass to collect warmth from the sun, the views from the main indoor entertaining areas—the first- and second-floor living rooms and dining area—would be just as important as the views from the garden itself. The land com-

Drawing upon English gardens for inspiration, Pamela Burton and Katie Spitz have created a Los Angeles garden (opposite) *in which the owner, a noted film director, enjoys working as well as entertaining. Violets and impatiens growing between the stones in the path introduce the garden color right at the terrace steps* (below).

prised fields overgrown with scrub trees and delineated by vine-covered walls. She cut through the dense undergrowth and was rewarded with an incredible view of the ocean across a tidal inlet. After taking full inventory of the site, McGuire found herself faced with the dilemma of deciding how much of the secondary growth to clear. Since this part of Rhode Island is historically an agricultural community, she decided to reclaim the fields and re-create the once-expansive vistas. This involved clearing most of the scrub and restoring many of the fields, saving the few fine existing trees. The architect sited the house so its walls of glass and many levels of decks took full advantage of the 180-degree views McGuire had revealed. She then began to shape the outdoor living spaces that were to include both terraces and decks.

First sculpting a gently curving bowl from the land directly adjacent to the lowest level of the house, McGuire then molded a bluestone terrace, which easily accommodates seating for thirty, into the bowl, where it is protected from the strong coastal winds. The resulting space is intimate and hidden from view; its gently curving walls of velvety lawn wrap around its inhabitants, creating an ideal place to entertain in the spring and fall, when the sun is warm yet the winds are still cool. The herbaceous border topping the rim echoes the curve of the terrace while

At this Rhode Island home, a deck adjacent to the master suite affords expansive views out over reclaimed fields (opposite). *To accommodate outdoor entertaining, Diane McGuire molded a bluestone terrace into the base of a gently curving bowl sculpted from the land* (below). *Protected from the steady coastal winds, it is an ideal space in which to entertain when the sun is warm and the winds are cool.*

providing accents of soft color. A lawn path with a more gradual slope leads up and out of the sheltered terrace area onto the expansive lawn, which is perfect for summer barbeques and large, informal parties. Further from the house, the clean edge of the mowing line defines the lawn, while an old fieldstone wall marks the point of transition to a controlled natural landscape with the ocean beyond.

This home is a true collaboration between architect and landscape architect. McGuire has sensitively created a landscape that is enjoyed as much from inside the house as outside, and every room has been designed by the architect to invite the outdoors into the house. Large, sliding glass doors open onto decks at both the first- and second-floor levels. From the first-floor living and dining areas, the glass doors frame the view of the colorful herbaceous border edging the terrace, the old stone walls separating the fields, and a slice of the tidal inlet. From the second-floor living room one feels as if on the bridge of a ship as the view from the deck is dramatically expanded: the ocean, hidden by sandbars on the lower levels, seems to come right into the house as if seen through a periscope. McGuire has opened up the views for both the lover of the sea and the gardener, and in the process has designed a landscape to be enjoyed year-round.

In contrast to these expansive East Coast views established by McGuire, Andrea and

Below: It is often impossible to avoid unattractive views from terraces, but espaliers can provide an excellent solution. Here, a creative gardener in Long Island's East Hampton espaliered apple trees in the Belgian-fence pattern to obscure his service entrance.

Opposite: When Lloyd Lawton designed this terrace and rock garden, he drew his inspiration from the rocky New England coast, which is within view.

84

All views are important in a backyard—those toward the house (opposite) as well as those from the house (below right). Since vegetable gardens and orchards often occupy large areas of a backyard, it is important that they be maintained to look attractive at all times, like these gardens in Vermont (far left) and East Hampton, New York (middle and below right).

86

Bruce Dern have created a small, private garden with narrowly focused views at their home in Malibu, California. Their vine-covered porch, adjacent to the living room, provides shade and forms a lovely, verdant frame for the garden paradise beyond. The beach, with all its activity, is edited from view. Only the ocean is visible through the white picket gate that Andrea designed. This is a charming, romantic backyard view, seemingly foreign to southern California. In the springtime the garden overflows with roses, such as Yolande and Mme. Alfred Carrière, accompanied by foxglove, lavender, delphinium, and iris. The porch is vibrant with a succession of climbing roses, bougainvillaea, and autumn clematis. A white birdhouse with a thatched roof, and another in the shape of a windmill, contribute to the cottage garden ambience. Although merely yards from the Pacific, looking out at this rich, personal garden transports the viewer to the English countryside.

If you are fortunate enough to have a spectacular panorama, your terrace should be sited to take full advantage of it. For an urban setting, however, it may be necessary to create a view by including a sculpture or fountain, thereby establishing an inward orientation. Los Angeles landscape architect Emmet L. Wemple utilizes sculptures and fountains as focal points as well as ways

At her Malibu, California home, Andrea Dern has created a charming, romantic backyard view, seemingly foreign to this heavily populated southern California location.

of leading people to the center of a garden setting.

For two art collectors in Portland, Oregon, an especially fulfilling experience comes by dining outside on their terrace surrounded by sculpture. When they inherited the house, which has been in the family for three generations, they commissioned Barbara Fealy to enlarge the outdoor living area and enhance the parklike garden. Fealy created a garden that showcases the sculpture while enhancing the views from the terraces, where the owners most often entertain. When dining in this fine garden one has a choice of views, expansive and bucolic, or intimate and specific as it is directed toward a David Botini sculpture, *Kachina Girl*, that is framed by a heavily pruned native hawthorn.

A parklike garden in Portland, Oregon was designed by Barbara Fealy both to showcase the owners' sculpture collection and to enhance the views from the entertaining areas. From the sitting area (below right), the view is of a bronze sculpture by Yu Ming, Tai Chi, *with the pool house in the distance. From the dining table (below left), the visitor is treated to a view of* Kachina Girl, *a sculpture by David Botini that is framed by a heavily pruned native hawthorn.*

TERRACES: OUTDOOR LIVING ROOMS

Terraces are often designed around two views: one distant and capacious, the other close and more immediate. A contemporary house with vast sunset views over Washington's Puget Sound embraces a large flagstone terrace with a central, raised, stone planter encasing a majestic old catalpa. The catalpa bestows a human scale on this substantial terrace while, in the warm summer months, the catalpa's

wide-spreading branches provide a cool, shaded place for lunch. In winter, yet another facet of this tree is revealed as its bare branches take on a wild sculptural quality. From the living room and dining room, Puget Sound is a lovely backdrop, and on days when the sound is obscured by fog or mist, the catalpa becomes an intriguing dark presence silhouetted against the grey veil.

Whether your terrace is large or small the addition of a special feature or lovely planting can provide year-round pleasure. This is particularly true when a terrace is enclosed on two or three sides by a house, making the terrace garden the focal point for the adjacent rooms.

Lloyd Lawton, a garden designer and stone mason, was asked to design and build a terrace within the purview of the two wings of a Rhode Island home, the garden of which was to be the focus from the living room. Upon entering, one's first impression would be influenced subtly by the view through the expansive glass windows. Understanding that whatever was in the foreground would need to be large enough to be thoroughly appreciated from the living room, Lawton designed a garden that incorporates large, local boulders at the base of which he tucked a lovely, natural fish pool.

Lawton set the tone for this exquisite terrace by employing softening ground-

Opposite: *An unusual variegated boxelder highlights the quiet sitting area of an intimate Seattle terrace* (top left). *Another Seattle garden lover has created an exquisite outdoor room by incorporating a ceiling of grapes, covered by another ceiling of plexiglass, and windows framed with elegant drapes and treillage* (top right): *a pleasant place to relax—rain or shine. On the other hand, a substantial bluestone terrace* (below, left and right) *easily accommodates parties for one hundred or more guests while its close relationship to the house and comfortable, oversized furniture make it an ideal space in which to entertain just a few. From intimate spaces for relaxation to lavish open areas for formal entertaining, terraces lend themselves to their owner's imaginative interpretations.*

Overleaf: *A majestic catalpa bestows a human scale on a large bluestone terrace with vast sunset views over Washington's Puget Sound.*

Below: *The low picket fence and yew hedge that enclose this brick terrace in Sagaponack, New York, offer separation from the lawn play area but still permit enjoyment of the view of the surrounding fields.*

91

covers, ferns, and low evergreens beneath a canopy of copper beech and Stewartia trees to contrast with hard boulders and the stone terrace. The owner, a highly regarded gardener, then contributed her own expertise: with bold strokes, she added the bright accents of color provided by lilies, irises, delphinium, *Lysimachia punctata*, *Corydalis lutea*, and other herbaceous plant materials, thus creating a small, constantly changing paradise and a delightful ambience for all her parties, no matter what the time of year.

Architects and landscape architects have joined forces in striving to achieve unity between house and garden. As architects incorporate more glass in the design of houses, gardens have been allowed to become an extension of the living space, both visually and in actuality. Today, terraces and decks are not only structural extensions of the home, but integral parts of the residents' lifestyle, and important backyard spaces in which to entertain one's friends.

A terrace often functions as an outdoor living room, and many of the same design criteria apply here that apply to the interior counterpart. To design a terrace on which to entertain one or fifty, it is important to create a space in which guests immediately feel at home and the conversation flows—a "room" with ample seating for intimate conversation as well as a large, open space

Designed for flexibility, this Seattle, Washington terrace is organized with several entertaining areas—two sitting areas, a dining area, and several single chaises set to the side for reading and relaxation.

where guests can mingle. On the other hand, an outdoor party also requires some degree of enclosure for definition in order to promote participation and to prevent the party from breaking up into little groups.

The surface of this area is the stage for the outdoor social event and should be in harmony with the house as well as the landscape. It must also take into account certain elements of entertaining that would be considered givens inside. For example, a terrace used for formal entertaining should have closely laid stone or brick to avoid snagging high heels. In creating her woodland gardens, Oregon landscape architect Barbara Fealy often uses finely crushed rock compacted with stone dust for walks and terraces. Most important, any horizontal surface, whether wood or stone, should be sound and level so that all furniture is stable. There are few things more annoying than the scramble for a pack of matches to steady a table just as the guests are about to arrive.

The shape of a terrace can add drama to a backyard of any size. The angularity of a contemporary-style home is enhanced by the strong, straight lines of a terrace, which are then reiterated by the meticulously maintained edge of the lawn; added interest comes with the contrast of curvilinear planting beds. Equally effective is the molding of a gently curving terrace into the contours of the surrounding backyard,

Below: *Steps and paths can at once control movement from an interior space and direct the eye. Here, a large fieldstone step acts as a visual link between indoors and out, while it also reflects the nearby stone wall, which is brought into focus by the French doors.*

thereby establishing a strong relationship with the landscape.

The size of a deck or terrace must relate directly to its function, and the architectural element should always be in scale with the house and landscape. For instance, in a small garden it is important to have a larger proportion of terrace to plantings. Sam and Elizabeth White have successfully prevented any feeling of claustrophobia in their urban garden by surrounding its relatively large, brick terrace with narrow beds of azaleas and ivy. The retaining wall at the rear of the garden has been disguised by a raised planting bed and seating wall.

Most important, the terrace or deck should be large enough to accommodate the number of guests most often entertained. A deck in Princeton, New Jersey, for example, was designed by James B. Baker for fifty-person sit-down dinners, where guests are seated at round tables for six and eight. If there is a rule of thumb to use in determining the appropriate size for a deck or terrace, it is: When in doubt, make it larger.

A gentle rain on a warm summer day can be delightful when witnessed from a comfortable armchair in the shelter of a porch or covered outdoor room. However, nothing puts an end to a garden party faster than an unexpected rain storm, and a roofed area adjacent to the terrace can be a real lifesaver.

Below and opposite: *The two wings of this Rhode Island house embrace the extraordinary water garden, which affords a serenely spectacular view from the living room.*

For weddings and large parties, a tent can always be rented in case the weather doesn't cooperate. In Seattle, a city known for its gentle mists and beautiful gardens, terraces are designed with covers that extend the season and offer shelter for comfortable, upholstered furniture. One terrace, which runs the entire length of a house overlooking Puget Sound in the Highlands, is divided into two sections: one open, the other partially enclosed. Abutting the living room, a plexiglas-covered arbor provides shelter from the elements while supplying a frame for the magnificent view. An extension of the interior space, the arbor room is furnished with an oversized wicker chaise, sofa, and armchairs as well as a wrought iron and glass dining table for four. Beneath a ceiling of grapes covered by plexiglas and within walls of lattice, windows framed by crisp, white curtains, and with a chandelier to cast a gentle glow, one feels as if one has entered the garden without leaving the luxurious comfort of the house.

For another Seattle hostess, who wanted to keep her garden open to the sky but still take no chances with the weather, a canopy of lightweight parachute cloth was the solution. The entire backyard, including the substantial terrace and the hillside garden, is spanned by yards of this wonderfully luminescent covering. Permanent hooks have been installed at the roof of the house

Opposite: The owners of this former sea-captain's cottage on Shelter Island truly appreciate the concept of indoor/outdoor living. When renovating their home, all first-floor rooms received French doors opening onto terraces.

For a Seattle hostess whose garden is central to all entertaining, evenings often begin on the terrace followed by candlelit dinners in the adjacent dining room. Lights hidden in the hillside softly accentuate the garden, which becomes the ethereal focus from the dining table.

and the far corners of the garden to facilitate installation. At night, lights hidden in the dense hillside plantings reflect off the white fabric, swathing the garden in a dramatic glow. Formal dinners on the terrace—with its surround of tall variegated box elders, rhododendrons, azaleas, perennials, and planters of cheerful annuals, all beneath this ethereal canopy—are magical and amaze guests with their comfort and beauty on otherwise rainy, grey evenings. When not in use, the parachute cloth can be folded and stowed in a closet.

Protection from the wind is the major consideration for cooler, more exposed gardens such as those in New England. Outdoor rooms with walls or hedges can create warm, sheltered microclimates within a larger garden space, encouraging the use of a garden earlier in the spring and later into the fall. One lover of spring flowering bulbs has enclosed an intimate terrace adjacent to the house with a five-foot-high brick wall. The wall retains heat from the sun while providing welcome protection from the wind. With this added warmth, the bulbs often bloom two weeks early. Every winter she looks forward to the sight of the first crocuses and snowdrops poking their heads out of the melting snow, for this is always the sign to begin planning her annual luncheon in the warm shelter of a garden surrounded by a joyous display of tulips, daffodils, and narcissus.

In small gardens, such as that belonging to the Samuel Whites of Manhattan, it is important to have a larger proportion of terrace to plantings to prevent feelings of claustrophobia.

Decks: Taking the Inside Out

In rugged terrain, decks are an effective way to extend outdoor entertaining areas out over the edge of a steep hillside. Constructed with a system of sturdy posts, framing, and wood flooring, decks are an excellent solution for an irregular site. They are especially useful in sensitive landscapes where it is unwise to interfere with the natural drainage of the area. The posts can be set to the side of a swale or a steep ravine, thus allowing for the uninterrupted flow of water off the site. At the same time, the decking obscures the unattractive, barren beds of ravines, which are dry most of the year and allow little to grow. Still another factor that recommends the construction of a deck is the way in which it favors existing trees: The post system is much less likely to damage the roots of trees than is the foundation of a terrace, and decks can also be worked around trees, extending the entertaining area out into the landscape. And the flooring can be laid in a number of ways to enhance the design. Diagonals, pinwheels, checkerboards—the combinations are limited only by the exterior dimensions.

The wood flooring also allows decks to be used year-round no matter what the climate. The spacing between the floor boards allows rain to run off and snow to

A deck designed by Emmet L. Wemple & Associates in Pacific Palisades, California functions to link all indoor and outdoor entertaining areas.

melt through the cracks. After an invigorating morning on the slopes, skiers find a hot lunch served on the deck of a chalet to be a special delight. Dining on a perch extended over the landscape, you feel as though you have never left the slopes.

Decks not only extend the usable area of a property but they often afford spectacular views. When designing a garden for a wine distributor in the hills above the Napa Valley, Jack Chandler used the many variations in terrain to heighten the great drama of the expansive view. Beginning at the front entrance, Chandler incorporated a series of decks that follow the slope, culminating in a panoramic view where the main deck projects out over the edge of the steep, rocky hillside. Whether entering directly from the drive or descending from the living room, guests always remember the initial thrill of looking out through the frame of live oaks at the impressive expanse of vineyards unfolding below. The spectacular view combined with the gentle dappled light of the live oaks sets just the right tone for lunches and early evening parties.

Like the brick terrace Burton and Spitz designed in Los Angeles, Gary Nacci's deck in Seattle, designed by Tim Holtschlag, is an extension of his home's interior space. However, since the deck is level with the first floor, it is a design that is practical only in areas where winters are not harsh or

Opposite: *The steps of this deck lead the visitor over a fragrant bed of lily of the valley.*

Decks are an excellent means of pushing the entertaining areas out into the treetops. A deck in Portland, Oregon (top) *has been manipulated around existing tree trunks and affords an excellent view of Mt. Hood. To blend their deck* (bottom left) *into the surrounding New England landscape, the owners enclosed it with a fieldstone wall, while Dutch Strawbridge utilizes his deck* (bottom right) *at grade to integrate both his pool and rose garden with his Rhode Island home.*

snowy. For a summerhouse, a home in California, or even in Seattle, where the climate most closely approximates that of England, it is not necessary to build the deck a step below the level of the house since snow is not likely to drift up against the door.

Nacci's deck directs the view to the adjacent Japanese-style garden with its sensitive use of plant materials in combination with water. To create a welcoming enclosure, Holtschlag set an evergreen hedge in wooden planters and disguised the embracing teahouse walls. A Japanese maple espaliered against the side fence is an extraordinary sight, and spring flowering bulbs and annuals ensure continuous color while the rhododendrons and azaleas bloom and even afterward. It is all punctuated by a small lily pond that delineates the transition to the woodland paradise beyond.

On the other hand, raised decks provide a new point of perspective from which to experience the garden. Free of obstructions like neighboring trees and hedges, raised decks are available to cooling summer breezes and once-hidden views. For homes built into hillsides, decks raised up to meet the living spaces project out over descending gardens, while those adjoining living and dining rooms provide the opportunity for easy movement from indoor to outdoor entertaining areas. Sliding glass doors pre-

Decks can provide ideal solutions for irregular sites, such as these overlooking Napa Valley (top left) *and the Willamette River* (top right). *For homes on hillsides, decks can permit easy access to the outdoors despite steep slopes; shown here* (bottom left) *is one in Portland, Oregon. They also establish gracious transitions as shown here* (bottom right) *in Seattle.*

sent a constant invitation to sample the deck's refreshing ambience. In Piedmont, California, a raised deck bordered by potted tangelo, lemon, and lime trees appeals to all the senses: Caressed by cool breezes, enfolded in the sweet fragrance of the citrus trees, distracted by hummingbirds seeking out the nectar, and soothed by the sound of doves that come to rest on the roof at dusk, it is an ideal place to relax on summer evenings.

To establish an illusion of spaciousness on steeply sloping hillside sites, raised decks can be utilized to project people into the landscape. One deck in Portland, Oregon is nestled in primeval forest. As the deck nestles around the massive trunks of Douglas fir trees, it entices guests to explore its farthest reaches, where they are rewarded with an extraordinary view out over the city toward Mount Hood. Guests feel at ease in the embrace of the towering, treehouselike limbs. With a built-in bench and a variety of moveable furniture, the deck requires little maintenance and is a natural place on which to entertain.

LAWNS: THE COUNTRYSIDE TAMED

Often the most important thread weaving a garden space together, lawns complement plantings in a formal garden as well as provide a soft surface for an informal

This lawn in Portland, Oregon is intended primarily for viewing, its lush green color acting as a lovely foil for the encompassing herbaceous border. Beginning with early white azaleas, the lawn and border cooperate to create a refreshing scene throughout most of the year.

children's play area. Wherever it may be, lush, green, manicured grass is always refreshing. Just the sight of a beautiful lawn conjures up wonderful thoughts of rolling country hillsides; even if just a patch in the city, it brings immediate pleasure to all who experience it. Not surprisingly, as velvet carpets for outdoor rooms or centerpieces in formal gardens, lawn terraces provide excellent surfaces on which to entertain. One such area in Los Angeles, designed by Walter Heideman of Emmet L. Wemple & Associates, is contiguous with the living room and easily accommodates a party for two hundred.

In New England, John Saladino uses a natural allée of tall maples accented by white birches for one of his outdoor entertaining spaces. What once may have been a cowpath now forms a natural transition between the formal terraces at the house and the woods beyond. On warm summer evenings, the host starts a party on the terrace, then leads his guests down into the allée, where a resplendent dinner awaits.

Lawn terraces, flush with hard-surface, outdoor entertaining areas, ease the crush of crowded parties and encourage guests to wander out into the garden. In Washington, D.C., a garden on two levels comprises both bluestone and lawn terraces: The bluestone terrace on the upper level abuts the house; it meets the first lawn terrace, which then leads one down steps

Opposite: *John Saladino's allée of tall maples accented by white birches forms a natural transition between the formal terrace at the house and the woods beyond.*

Below: *At the top of a promontory, the bench along the edge of this lawn terrace also marks a steep drop-off. By making a cut through the pine-covered peninsula, the owners were able to capture a dramatic vista of a distant lighthouse.*

with risers of granite and treads of grass to the other. This imaginative use of grass allows for uninterrupted movement throughout the garden.

Many gardeners have found that cutting back leads to surprises, and this technique was put to good use for a lawn terrace in Rhode Island. Neighboring the living and dining rooms, the terrace was enclosed on two sides by an old fieldstone wall buried in years of overgrowth. When the owners of the house began to cut back the mounds of vines and uncover the walls, they found many of the original fifty-year-old perennials. Reinforced with masses of bright annuals and additional perennials, an exuberant herbaceous border was formed that is a riot of color all summer long. They also uncovered a birdbath—now a focal point in the garden—and an old stone path that bisects the lawn.

While many would consider a stone path to be an intrusion in the lawn terrace, the owners chose to incorporate it into the overall design of the garden. By planting the path with cheerful flowering thyme and sedum, they have infused the lawn with color while visually dividing it into two distinct entertaining spaces. The two lawn areas are furnished in ways that permit their functioning both separately or as a larger whole: One has less-formal groupings of chaises and tables, while the other houses a wrought iron and glass table for

Opposite: *Protected from the winter winds, lunches in this garden designed by Isabelle C. Greene in the hills above Santa Barbara are always pleasant and warm. In summer, however, the wide porch offers welcome relief from the scorching sun.*

Below: *Lawns, like this one in Rhode Island, are often the most important thread weaving through a garden space.*

109

six. The hostess serves her guests a glass of wine at a table overlooking the flower beds and orchard to get parties off to a lively start. She then likes to move across the path for dinner and the expansive view of the sun setting over orchard and field.

When the view is the main feature of the garden, a lawn terrace will act as its foil. Such a lawn terrace atop a promontory on the coast of New England was designed to take full advantage of the panoramic views. A continuous wood bench at its edge directs the eye out toward a faraway, pine-covered peninsula. By cutting a swath through the pines, the owners have permitted a vista to a distant lighthouse on an island at the mouth of the harbor.

In Portland, Oregon, however, it was the lawn terrace itself that was carved out of a primeval forest. Whereas a deck might project one out into the treetops, here the entertaining area is at ground level, within the domain of the massive trunks of the native fir and maple trees. Dwarfed by their great height, one experiences fully the grandeur of the landscape.

Here landscape architect Barbara Fealy has sculpted the woods to create the vistas, which are integral to this garden, through a process of cutting away. She has achieved a grand expanse with intimate spaces hidden within the great sweeps of native shrubs and rhododendrons. With its great con-

trasts of scale, this garden is at once other-worldly and peaceful.

THE OUTDOOR KITCHEN

The backyard garden is an ideal location for outdoor dining, and an outdoor kitchen lends greatly to the pleasure of backyard entertaining. However, whether you want a small hibachi hidden in the far corner of a city terrace or a gas cooker hooked up to the house, it is wise to consider the needs of outdoor cooking when first beginning to plan or revitalize the garden. Each type of outdoor grill has specific requirements directly related to its source of fuel: Storage for charcoal is just as important a consideration as the source of fuel for a gas cooker; and, though integrating an underground gasline from the house to a permanent grill eliminates the hassles of refilling gas tanks, this decision will also have significant impact on situating the equipment.

The prevailing wind is another major consideration when locating grills and hook-ups for gas cookers. Although the aromas emanating from the grill are apt to be mouthwatering, the smoke can easily envelop a terrace to disastrous effect. It is therefore best to locate stationary outdoor grills downwind of the primary entertaining areas but not far from the kitchen. In addition, since cooking always attracts a

Pages 110–111: A magnificent lawn was sculpted out of this primeval forest just seven minutes from downtown Portland, Oregon. Walls of massive Douglas firs and native maples render this garden at once serene and otherwordly. On the other hand, to bring an intimate scale to the otherwise grand landscape, native shrubs and groundcovers such as Salal, Oregon grape, and Kinnikinnick have been included along with rhododendrons and a small fish pool.

Upon entering this very special herb garden, the delicious scent of the fresh thyme, which grows between the stones, is unleashed, stimulating all senses.

crowd, placing tables and chairs near the grill encourages guests to take part. Lightweight furniture is best used near a grill, however, since the wind can change without warning. A table next to the grill provides a welcome rest for utensils and serving dishes. Most of all, for those who cook out on a regular basis, the outdoor kitchen should be convenient to its indoor counterpart in order to accommodate an easy transit of food, drink, and utensils.

The best gardens for outdoor dining generally have been designed around the type of outdoor cooking the hosts enjoy most. For one Vermont couple who prefer charcoal, the grill has been built into a wall bordering a bluestone kitchen terrace overlooking their pond, the mountains providing a spectacular backdrop. Since fresh herbs are essential to preparing most meals, they have planted a lovely herb garden right next to the terrace, allowing the fragrances and colors to stimulate the senses gently in preparation for the gastronomic delights to follow.

Colorful mixtures of flowers and herbs planted in terra cotta pots enhance any kitchen garden and can easily be brought inside for use during the winter. Many flowers are edible: for example, nasturtiums, which always look cheerful in the garden, add a brilliant orange accent and a pleasant peppery sharpness to a salad of

With an herb garden on one side, a charcoal grill built into the wall on the other, and a sunset view over the mountains, this Vermont terrace is an outdoor chef's dream.

mixed greens. Lemon Gem marigolds, with their clear yellow color and lemon-verbenalike scent, are a lovely addition to chicken or vegetable dishes, while the lavender blossoms of chives have been used since Roman times in the preparation of egg or cheese dishes that require a subtle onion flavor.

In John Saladino's kitchen garden, the potted plants have been carefully selected for taste, color, and fragrance. Placed at four different levels, they create a wall of color that diverts attention from the Weber grill and provides an especially beautiful view from the kitchen windows.

Unlike a Weber grill, a barbeque pit cannot be rolled out of the way for large parties. Most often constructed of field-stone or brick, it becomes the central element wherever it is built. A fieldstone barbeque pit in northwestern Connecticut has been hidden in its own garden room carved out of the woods. Here it is the focus of the garden room and the generator of all activity in the garden. In keeping with the scale of the surrounding woods it is imposingly large, so the owners take great pleasure in decorating this outdoor kitchen for each occasion in order to create a more intimate scale. For luncheons, the picnic tables might be adorned with wildflowers while hanging baskets filled with cheerful annuals are suspended from the overhanging branches. For evening entertaining,

Opposite: Terra cotta pots of colorful flowers and herbs enhance a kitchen garden and distract the eye from the Weber grill hidden in the corner. Although this garden is not intended specifically for entertaining, it is certainly a lovely place to be while dinner sizzles nearby.

For a Portland couple who wanted to encourage their guests to venture out into the garden, Barbara Fealy designed a deck that is accessible from each adjacent room of the house.

In Piedmont, California, a deck added off the living room is high above the neighboring hedgerow and open to the cooling summer breezes.

the baskets could be replaced by Chinese lanterns which shed a gentle glow.

For a home in Princeton, New Jersey, the barbeque pit was integrated into the design of the house. Constructed of the same brick, it is enclosed by a sitting wall—an extension of the house—and is sheltered by a roof echoing that of the main house. The proximity to the house and the protection from the elements inspires the owners to use this barbeque pit regularly throughout the year.

Unfortunately, many barbecue pits can be as unattractive as they are imposing. When one must be added close to the house, care should be taken to ensure that it is not a focus when seen from the house. Setting it off to one side or placing it within an attractive garden shelter can feature a more pleasing scene within the frame of the windows and terrace doors.

A good example of this approach is a sheltered garden room in Seattle that combines an outdoor kitchen and living area in elegant style. Open on three sides to the terrace and garden, the back wall comprises a brick fireplace and built-in gas grill. Furnished with two overstuffed chaises, it is an inviting retreat most of the year.

An elegant garden structure can camouflage unattractive outdoor grills. This garden room in Seattle, Washington—with its built-in grill and fireplace, and its overstuffed chaises—is an inviting retreat throughout most of the year.

INSPIRATION FOR ENTERTAINMENT

The garden can provide inspiration for the most memorable parties. Flowering trees, birds and butterflies, the harvest of fruit and vegetables, all contribute to the garden's ambience, but they also can—and should—influence the hosts' initial decisions when organizing a social event. For example, a party could be scheduled for the week when a certain flower is in bloom or fruit is harvested. Or the color scheme for the linens and plates might be chosen to coordinate with the dominant color of an herbaceous border at a particular time.

A glorious cherry tree in full bloom inspired a luncheon in late May that was "a celebration of pink." Our hostess moved a round antique dining room table outside and placed it beneath the spreading branches of the cherry tree. She then set a most exquisite table all in pink using china and crystal that had been in her husband's family for generations. Surrounded by glowing pink blossoms gently falling in the ocean breeze, backlit by the brilliant sun, we enjoyed a delicious lunch, also predominantly pink: poached salmon in a light mousseline, Salade Violette—a composition of endive, watercress, and pink violets concocted by our hostess just for this occasion—and a tart of fresh cherries and apricots.

A deck off the master suite allows the owners of this East Hampton garden to enjoy their flowering cherry tree at all levels. When the tree is in full bloom, comfortable upholstered chairs are brought outdoors just for the occasion and breakfasts tend to last all morning.

Not surprisingly, backyard entertaining in the Napa Valley revolves around wine, especially at harvest time, and gardens here are often designed to take advantage of the extraordinary views. Terraces overlook rows of brilliant green grapevines, which appear to extend for miles before intersecting with the embracing hills, thereby enhancing the experience of enormous depth. Parties on these terraces are often quiet, informal affairs. Sipping wine and relaxing in the caress of a gentle breeze, guests are mesmerized by the vineyard as it sparkles in the California sun.

Grapes also set the tone for a party in North Seattle. Inspired by the heavy bunches of grapes hanging from the arbor shading her formal terrace, one hostess holds an annual wine-tasting party when the grapes have reached their peak. Big brass buckets holding bottles of wine are placed strategically around the terrace. Guests are encouraged to wander through the many exquisite gardens while sipping the wine and enjoying the sculpture and fountains.

When Jack Chandler designed his own garden in the Napa Valley, an existing olive tree became the inspiration for developing his concept: a garden with an Italian accent. To one side of the olive tree, Chandler built an entrance courtyard and reading patio; to the other, a pergola-shaded terrace and swimming pool were added as his pri-

Harvest time is the inspiration for many late-summer parties in John Saladino's vegetable and cutting garden.

mary entertaining area. Stepping onto the terrace, guests are surrounded by fabulous, waist-high ornamental grasses. Water-spouts projecting from a nearby stone wall provide a continuous splashing murmur that is enhanced by the gentle rustling of the grasses, establishing a wonderfully re-laxing and romantic ambience. Italian terra cotta olive-oil urns, filled with grasses, soften the rectilinear lines of the pool and terrace. For one party, Chandler took the Italian theme all the way: He set up tables and chairs on the lawn next to the pool and employed tablecloths and decorations all in green, red, and white. To complete the mood, violinists and accordion players wandered through the garden as the guests danced and dined late into the night.

The *lack* of a terrace inspired one very memorable evening near Newport, Rhode Island. The hostess, searching for a birth-day present for her husband, decided to give him a new terrace garden. While he was off on a business trip, she had a big white tent set up around the site for the new terrace and went to work. In only two days she had the walls rebuilt and added a fence, planted hundreds of annuals and perennials, and installed a birdhouse and a sculpture just in time for his return. As he entered the tent on his birthday, he began to believe in miracles: It had become a fairyland—a beautiful new backyard garden filled with all his favorite people.

Opposite: *Jack Chandler designed this terrace in Napa Valley to take full advantage of the extraordinary views. Looking out across the tops of brilliant green grapevines, guests are mesmerized by the vineyard as it sparkles in the California sun.*

Chapter 4

Urban Delights

Whether an apartment's backyard or a penthouse in the ether, the urban garden is an oasis that provides the ideal setting for any social occasion. City gardens large and small supply welcome relief from often claustrophobic urban conditions. They can include refreshing spaces in which to entertain, a play area for children, and an ideal spot for summer cookouts. The sound of birds attracted by city plantings can transport you mentally to the country, while a fish pool dotted with koi can call up images of the Orient.

Formal or informal, the goal in such a garden is to achieve a space that feels private yet not closed in. As landscape architect Alice Pickman says, "the most important ingredients of a successful urban garden design are scale, proportion, and logic." A city garden should give the appearance of openness and depth. In a long, narrow lot, a feeling of transition and distance can be created by connecting two terraces with a curving path or a set of steps. The impression of movement through space can be produced by repeating the use of a particular plant along a path or wall. Incorporating curvilinear lines in a limited garden space heightens the visual excitement, while straight lines are more formal.

City conditions always provide a great challenge to any garden owner. Air pollution and sufficient sunlight are major considerations in townhouse gardens, while wind, building structure, and excessive sunlight are important considerations for rooftop gardens. In city gardens, it is important to be aware of microclimates caused by wind and temperature fluctuations. For a rooftop garden, always consider the distance of the terrace from the ground—the higher the floor, the cooler the microclimate. In some cases there can be an entire climate zone's difference, which is critical in making intelligent plant selections. Surrounding buildings can also severely influence the wind currents as well as light. In cities with high pollution levels, one may find it necessary to clean soot regularly off the leaves of shrubs and trees to prevent the blocking of the stomates through which the plants breathe. A city environment is controlled, not natural. One must, therefore, assure a source for water and, in most cases, for its drainage as well. All of these conditions must be taken into consideration when choosing the plant materials. Most important, the plants should provide year-round interest since the garden will, in most cases, become the view from the interior living area.

A city garden brings life to the interiors of townhouses or apartments. With the addition of French doors, large windows, or a greenhouse enclosure, a small apartment can be made to appear twice its size by enhancing the visual ties to an adjacent garden. In providing the opportunity to walk outside into a verdant, private space, urban gardens encourage a feeling of freedom that soothes and relaxes.

OUTDOOR ROOMS

Outdoor rooms represent the merging of architecture and landscape. Fences, hedges, or walls enclose and define the room. Verdant ceilings comprising branching trees or vine-covered pergolas provide shelter and privacy, while the floors of stone or grass are, as Diane McGuire suggests, "an idiom." She goes on to explain that, "in an outdoor room in the country, the more grass area the better. In the city, hard surfaces are more suitable. It is best to treat the garden floor in the city as a true floor."

The garden rooms that follow are wonderfully private spaces in which to entertain, read, and simply appreciate the pleasures of the natural surroundings. They may be furnished as an outdoor extension of

Below and opposite: *To create an impression of greater space and provide a variety of experiences, this garden behind a Manhattan townhouse was divided into two distinct areas: a brick terrace on grade and a gravel terrace one step higher. A raised planting bed serves as the focus from both, allowing for a secluded walk on the far side of the garden. A collection of sculpture adds year-round interest.*

the house, with comfortable chairs for lounging and tables for dining. Or they may be open, with a central focus such as a sculpture or fountain and extensive plantings around the perimeter.

At the Carrington House in Providence, Rhode Island, landscape architect Lydia Jastramm transformed a dark, ivy-smothered side yard into an outdoor living room. A very private space, this garden room is totally enclosed with an inward focus toward a bright-green carpet of grass and a lovely, small fish pool. As guests enter the garden from the house, they initially walk onto a flagstone landing, where they must then turn to follow steps to the terrace below. The symmetrical paths lead first toward intimate alcoves then around flowering pear trees to the inviting, sun-drenched gravel terrace. When one sits on the terrace, the surrounding brick walls disappear into the shadows and the landing is hidden by a mass of azaleas and rhododendrons.

The imposing structure of enclosing brick walls for an outdoor room can be naturally softened by training climbing vines or espaliered shrubs and trees against their massive expanses. At the Carrington House, an espalier provides both the backdrop for the sitting area and a focus for guests as they enter the garden from the house. Their gaze stops at the wall, never

The creation of the walled garden at Carrington House (ca. 1810) in Providence, Rhode Island, was part rediscovery and part restoration. Lydia Jastramm's goal was to dig out the existing garden to provide the physical and visual experiences afforded by changing levels. In doing so, she uncovered the huge stone plates over the cistern (below right), *which mark the level of the original garden designed 150 years earlier, a level that ironically coincided with her own plan. The surrounding brick walls* (right) *are graced with elegant espaliers of flowering crab-apples, viburnums, and climbing hydrangeas.*

continuing into the neighboring yard, and the resulting ambience is one of utter calm and complete privacy.

To provide variety within the limited perimeters of a garden room in Washington, D.C.'s Georgetown, Oehme, van Sweden and Associates divided the space into two distinct areas. One, with a hard-surfaced floor of red brick, is set up for entertaining. The other has a carpet of green lawn. In this garden, which spans the distance between the owners' home and a smaller building, each of the areas is multifunctional. The lawn terrace is ideal as the children's play area while it also provides added space for large parties. The other half of the garden contains the terrace as well as a swimming pool large enough for swimming laps but shallow enough for children. Painted black, it becomes a reflecting pool when not inhabited by swimmers or splashers. This stunning garden room is as perfect for formal parties as it is for barbeques.

Oehme, van Sweden and Associates have designed here a most visually exciting garden. The large fields of color, which define the separate activity areas, are incorporated into an overall composition of green (the lawn), red (the brick), and black (the pool), all tied together by bold diagonal lines of limestone edging. This use of a strong diagonal expands the space while leading the eye into the garden, and serves

Pages 127–129: *In this Washington, D.C. garden, Oehme, van Sweden and Associates employed illusionistic concepts to expand the limited garden space visually. Strong diagonal patterns effect a perception of greater distance between points. The decorative brick wall and planting at the end of the pool provide a lovely focus for swimmers while disguising the pool-cover equipment.*

as a counterpoint to the extraordinary textures of the surrounding plants.

Entering the garden directly from the street through the original brick gateway arch, a guest's first step is onto the rich carpet of meticulously maintained grass. The tamed wildness of the garden in the distance entices the visitor to bypass the formal living room entrance and to explore the garden further. Color and texture are everywhere. Spikes of liatris and bamboo rise above clumps of ornamental grasses. Wisteria and silverlace vine rise above borders of ligularia and nandina, hosta, loosestrife and hardy hibiscus. The wonderfully wild tangle of wisteria and silverlace vine continues along the top of the high brick wall providing a lush ceiling molding around this spacious outdoor room. In spring, the garden is aglow with hundreds of tulip blooms. Summer evening poolside cookouts are casually elegant as the pool reflects all that cascades over its edges. Installed behind a Japanese maple, amidst ornamental grasses and rudbeckia, a gas grill is convenient yet unobtrusive. Dining on the terrace, the smoky aroma permeating the air and grasses rustling all around, the visitor is transported far from the hubbub of city life.

When the William H. Drapers moved to Georgetown from California, they also called upon Oehme, van Sweden and Asso-

Below and opposite: *Lap pools can be both functional and ornamental. Painted black, this lap pool is the centerpiece of another Washington, D.C. garden designed by Oehme, van Sweden and Associates. The white staircase—which is elegantly reflected in the pool's mirrorlike surface—was added to facilitate the gracious flow of guests from indoor to outdoor entertaining areas.*

ciates to design a garden room. Unlike the modern canvas of the previous garden, this one was to be rooted in the architectural traditions of Georgetown, yet versatile enough for the Drapers to continue the indoor/outdoor California lifestyle they so enjoyed. They wanted a private and personal garden space that would be both an extension of their indoor living area and capable of easily accommodating large parties.

First, brick walls were added to provide privacy from the adjacent street and to give definition to the garden room. The red bricks blended in with the traditional architecture of Georgetown while also swathing the garden in a warm reflective glow. In the cooler months the bricks retain heat from the sun, enabling the Drapers to entertain on the terrace earlier in the spring and later into the fall.

Tucked away behind the high brick wall is a large outdoor room with a handsome black lap pool as its focus. Surrounding the pool is a brick terrace with a colorful border of perennials and evergreen shrubs. Here, the designers have achieved the year-round lush look that is so effortless in California, creating a lovely ambience in which to entertain outdoors. To facilitate an easy flow of people from house to garden, a dining room entrance was enlarged and a wide, white wooden stairway was added to a living room balcony, its classic lines reflecting elegantly in the pool.

Built on two levels, with a small dining alcove off to one side, the garden design comprises a number of long views, which enhance the feeling of spaciousness. Passing through the garden's front gate, the guest arrives at the entrance terrace several feet above the main entertaining area. Seeing the dramatic view of the garden through a frame of arching branches of a picturesque weeping willow, one is naturally encouraged to join the party on the terrace below.

The Pastoral Urban Landscape

For some, the outdoor room provides the perfect opportunity to bring a touch of the country into the city. Isolated from the more urban elements of its setting, an outdoor room can be transformed with imaginative combinations of structures and plants, furniture and ornament. Vegetables and herbs, a picket fence or a rock outcropping—all are unexpected and establish a casual, country ambience within an urban garden.

On historic College Hill in Providence, Rhode Island, an area of architecturally fine homes with small front and side lots, landscape architect Lydia Jastramm transformed a garden that was overgrown with weeds into a small, countrylike paradise. Within the confines of a high wooden

Lydia Jastramm brought the country into the city with this Providence, Rhode Island garden. Stepping-stone paths, rustic fences, flower and vegetable gardens, large areas of lawn, and corners left to be wild and mysterious were all combined to evoke images of rural, New England countryside. The Bermuda bench, nestled in shrubs shaded by the wide-spreading branches of apple trees, becomes a magical place for the children to play on summer days.

fence, she sculpted the existing hillside into a series of outdoor rooms. Upon opening the front gate, a visitor is drawn into the garden by a view of a Bermuda bench nestled beneath the sheltering limbs of a wide, old apple tree. An open lawn with perennial borders, a picturesque vegetable garden surrounded by a rustic fence, and a small garden house further enhance the "rural" atmosphere. Grass-covered ramps and a series of stone steps lead to the dining terrace on the upper level, adjacent to the kitchen. The corners of the garden have been left natural, ever-changing, and mysterious. During the early summer, when the apple tree is in full bloom and the perennial border is bursting with color, all those held in the garden's thrall are relaxed by the harmony and beauty of the lush surroundings. They are gently permitted to forget completely the garden's urban setting.

For a couple living just outside of Boston, Alice Pickman designed a sixty-by-fifty-foot garden of rocks and woodland plants with a lovely waterfall, to infuse their day with the delights of a country setting. Through the terrace doors of the breakfast and dining rooms, the view is suggestive of an inviting clearing in the woods. A rich, velvety green lawn is bordered by gently curving beds of perennials and flowering evergreen shrubs with a

In the greater-Boston area, Alice Pickman designed a garden where rocks, ferns, birches, and hemlocks encompass a luxuriant lawn (opposite) *reminiscent of a forest clearing. The gently gurgling waterfall* (below) *provides the garden's focus while masking the sounds of nearby traffic.*

Whitespire Japanese birch marking the beginning of a seemingly natural stream. Birds splash in the small pool at the terminus, and the hemlocks and pines of a neighboring garden provide an effective backdrop.

For those dining on the deck, the ambience created gives the feeling of being in a garden of great depth, far from its urban setting. The shrub border juts into the lawn, placing large foreground elements within the view from the table. In contrast, the waterfalleapp ars to be very far away, when in actuality the distance is less than forty feet. Looking down across sculptural groupings of rocks, ferns, bleeding heart, astilbe, and a wide variety of azaleas and groundcovers, the sounds of the city obscured by the flowing water, one's thoughts are focused completely on the pleasures of this refreshing garden.

For some, the country becomes exotic. In another Georgetown backyard garden, Oehme, van Sweden and Associates created a junglelike paradise, combining flowing ornamental grasses with a splash of large-leaved magnolias, dense masses of shrubs, and accents of flowering perennials, all mixed together beneath towering native trees. Looking out from the shade of the porch, the feeling is one of being on safari—or perhaps more aptly, having been magically installed in a painting by Rous-

seau—not that of close proximity to the White House. With its dense plantings and rustling grasses, the garden is especially evocative when softly lit for evening parties.

For Richard Anderson the challenge was not fencing his neighbors out but convincing them to join in. Once this was done, Anderson had the backyards of six townhouses at his disposal, and he has created a marvelous, informal country garden for himself and his neighbors in the center of Albany, New York. Designed to include such private, separate spaces as terraces close to the townhouses, the gardens begin to flow from one into another as the visitor walks out from the buildings. Strolling within this limited space, measuring 120 by 110 feet, is like being on a marvelous journey. Mysterious corners were created; around each, another sensory delight is revealed: here is a rock garden with a small goldfish pool, then a vegetable garden; next is a lovely Italian garden planted all in silver and gold, beyond are arbors and a gazebo. Over five hundred varieties of trees, shrubs, perennials, groundcovers, and climbing vines are imaginatively combined to weave a wonderful tapestry of leaf patterns and textures. Anderson has created an extraordinary country garden that permits great tranquility within its urban environment.

Shaded by towering trees, five-foot-high ornamental grasses combine with the large, glossy leaves of magnolias and rhododendrons to conjure up visions that are as exotic when viewed from the house (below right) *as when enjoyed from the terrace hidden in the depths of this Washington, D.C. garden* (opposite) *designed by Oehme, van Sweden and Associates. A* fountain *(below), which is adjacent to the porch, distracts attention from sounds coming from the neighbor's garden on the other side of the wall.*

Overleaf: *Behind six townhouses in downtown Albany, New York, Richard Anderson has created a wonderfully tranquil refuge in which small, private areas near the houses open onto interconnecting garden spaces. Whereas birdbaths, a fishpool, an Italian garden punctuated by decorative urns, pedestals and architectural artifacts, and a rustic gazebo all contribute to the experience of this extraordinary urban garden, the rich green lawn is the thread that ties all these lovely elements together.*

Illusion in the Garden

One way to solve design problems caused by space limitations in city gardens is to work magic. Mirrors provide the illusion of greater depth as they reflect the garden itself. Lattice—constructed with cleverly calculated angles—can alter the eye's perception of a space, tricking it into perceiving great depth.

Alice Pickman worked magic in two gardens in Cambridge, Massachusetts. The first was created within a space only twenty feet wide and three times as long between the house and the neighbor's concrete-block garage. To disguise the unattractive garage and to give the illusion of increased depth, she re-created a Japanese scene. A bluestone path leads from the street, past what appears to be the entrance to a Japanese warehouse, to its end at a small, white-marble-chip terrace. Pickman has hidden the garage behind a false facade that includes a shallow porch and peaked roof. Around the terrace a raised planter provides another layer of interest when viewed from the adjacent screened porch. The planting of fastigiate white pines and yellow bamboo enhances the Japanese spirit while diminishing the height of the encompassing fence. Vertical logs of white cedar were used to curve the planting bed gently around the terrace within the tight

Opposite: Mirrors can work magic to overcome limitations within urban gardens. The view from the second floor of this Manhattan townhouse "through" the archway is fascinating—so much so that the less-than-attractive apartment building beyond is ignored. From the first floor, the garden appears to go on forever thanks to this reflective sleight-of-hand. A false front (below) is also an effective way to disguise unappealing views and to expand a space visually. In Cambridge, Massachusetts, Alice Pickman has imaginatively disguised a neighbor's concrete-block garage so that it resembles a Japanese warehouse.

confines of this urban space. Looking out from the house fills visitors with delight as this garden transports them to the courtyard gardens of Japan.

Mrs. Pickman next tackled a dark, tree-shaded garden, with only thirty feet between the floor-to-ceiling music room window and the neighbor's dilapidated stockade fence. Once again, the landscape architect chose to utilize illusion to overcome the not-inconsiderable constraints. The theme, again Japanese, was a re-creation in miniature of the view of a mountain as seen from a temple in Japan. She has compressed the landscape, which rises vertically in layers as in Japanese paintings, and the "mountain" screens the neighbor's junglelike backyard.

To provide a healthy growing environment for the garden, Pickman first removed several existing hemlocks to increase light levels. Then, the designer created a new landscape by constructing a cribbing retaining wall that was then filled with soil. Massive rocks found in a field in central Massachusetts were lifted by crane over the house and into position. Japanese maples, white birch, bamboo, and ferns were then planted on the resulting berm. Highlighted against the rocks and the matte leaves of hemlocks and rhododendrons, the shimmering leaves of the shade-tolerant plants lead the eye up the "mountain," and a waterfall brings it back

For another Cambridge garden, this one just thirty feet deep, Alice Pickman re-created a serene view from a temple in Japan—in miniature.

down to where the water splashes on a bed of glossy, black stones. Now a peaceful and beautiful "mountain view" dominates the music room, transporting one to the tranquil, picturesque setting of the Japanese temple that served as inspiration for the garden.

A fountain made from a millstone fills the space with a deep, resonant sound, while it entices birds into this Washington, D.C. garden. For visitors sitting in the adjacent family room, the fountain—now at eye level—affords a delightful view any time of year.

CITY SANCTUARY

Usually small, townhouse gardens are miniature urban oases squeezed in between adjacent buildings and abutting gardens. Privacy is a major consideration since these gardens often share common walls. The design of a townhouse garden is closely integrated with that of the interior entertaining spaces, thereby allowing these gardens to provide refreshing, verdant views from specific windows and doors along with all the pleasures of a private outdoor retreat.

When architect Sam White and his wife, Elizabeth, moved into a New York City townhouse, their small garden was dark, dirty, and gloomy. Nevertheless, White was convinced that it could become an important extension of their living space, an outdoor room in which to enjoy an evening drink with friends or spend a quiet afternoon with the children.

With the creative use of raised brick planters, a lattice fence, and rhodo-

dendrons and ivy, White disguised the massive stone retaining wall and the substantial difference in elevation. A hawthorn tree provides privacy from above. Seen from the dining table are terra cotta pots overflowing with geraniums and vinca, providing a colorful accent and enticing guests out through the French doors and up into the garden. White has transformed this once unattractive lot and has provided a delightful focus for their eat-in kitchen and a view from the upstairs living room.

Another Oehme, van Sweden and Associates garden in Georgetown again divides the entertaining areas, here providing a sunny dining terrace to complement the intimate sitting area, all within the limits of a narrow, sloping property abutting a townhouse. Conceived as two separate entertaining areas within one outdoor room, the dining terrace fits neatly into a corner formed by the townhouse's living and dining rooms, while the sitting area is set apart, up on the slight hillside, sheltered by a ceiling of wide-branching crabapple and magnolia trees. The stepping-stone path leads through iris, potentilla, lady's-mantle, lamb's-ears, and silver mound, past a stand of young bamboo and a gently flowing fountain made from an old millstone, to the cool shade of the sitting area. Hidden around the corner, in a dense planting of mountain laurel, is a small bench just for the grandchildren. They can

Having used French doors to establish a strong visual link (opposite), *the New York City garden of the Samuel White family has become an inviting extension of their indoor living space.*

Found objects, such as "lucky" stones and shells, carefully placed amidst the plantings surrounding this New York City penthouse, distract attention from the Brutalist architecture of the neighboring Whitney Museum.

be close by while their grandparents are entertaining on the terrace, yet feel as if they are in a secret world all their own. Luncheons on the terrace are always refreshing. Enveloped by the rich sound of water spilling over the edge of the millstone into a hollow drum obscured by beautifully rounded stones, mixed with those of the chirping and splashing of birds playing in the fountain, one feels far removed from the frenetic pace of the capital district.

GARDENS IN THE SKY

What better way to escape the noise, speed, and high energy of the city than to retreat to an aerie? Creating such a rooftop refuge is a real challenge, however. Not only must the wind be taken into account, but so too must other considerable factors such as neighboring buildings, light, and views. All furniture, planters, and garden ornaments must either be secured to the terrace or heavy enough to withstand high winds. Then factor in the reality that since rooftops are designed to accommodate only a specific load, weight must also become an important consideration.

When all these problems can be overcome, however, roof terraces can be wonderfully successful. When the elevator doors open into Dawn Mello's Manhattan penthouse, one is greeted with an exquisite vision of a garden room that could be set in

To step out onto Abbie Zabar's Manhattan terrace, the wind in your hair and Central Park stretching out far below, is to enter a fantasy high in the city sky. Fabulous swirls of juniper reach toward the sun, and potted herbal topiaries, all created by Abbie herself (she is the author of The Potted Herb)*, fill the air with a wonderful blending of aromas.*

Regency England. Elegant, green-wire period furniture made plush with colorful cushions is nestled among pots of pink cleome and sedum, yellow coreopsis, geraniums, and herbs. Surrounded by shrubbery walls of arborvitae, euonymous capped with showy, autumn-blooming clematis, and pyracantha trained with roses, this terrace is a delightfully private space in which to entertain. The shrubbery, as conceived by Perry Guillot, not only defines the space but blocks the view from nearby buildings. On summer evenings, guests move easily through the living room doors onto the adjacent terrace. The cool greens and cheerful colors are a refreshing contrast to the monotone city skyline.

With the imaginative incorporation of planters, tall honey locust and birch trees, bright white trelliswork, and a number of different floor treatments, John and Gwen Burgee have created a series of gardens in a spectacular New York City setting. These are urban oases that transport all those within their embrace far from the cares of daily life.

The entrance to the rooftop garden is through a greenhouse. Burgee has designed an interesting variation here: a loggia, with an Oriental carpet on the floor, serves as an entry hall. This intimate space, with its view of planters overflowing with

Below and opposite: Dawn Mello's Manhattan penthouse terrace evokes images of Regency England. Terra cotta pots filled with flowers, herbs, and even tomatoes define the dining and sitting areas while hedges and an awning overhead work together to obscure neighboring buildings.

flowers chosen for continuous bloom, sets the tone for the garden that is yet to unfold.

The neighboring red-tiled terrace is open and devoid of furniture, making it ideal for parties, and a gravel terrace off to the side accommodates any overflow. Here, Gwen Burgee has filled planters with mugo pines, daylilies, and dahlias to provide a lush natural border. The view down this penthouse terrace toward the formal water garden and lattice wall beyond seems to stretch to forever.

Drawn by a gently flowing fountain, a lily pond, and an alluring lattice arbor designed by Burgee, the exploring guest moves on to discover what lies hidden behind the lattice wall. Surrounded by silvery artemesia while walking down a stepping-stone path, in light dappled by the branches of honey locust trees, one is filled with a sensuous tranquility. Passing into the enclosure of the vaulted lattice arbor, one seems to be entering the vestibule of a very special secret garden. With its fern-filled planters and cool shade, it provides a refreshing interlude, evoking woodland scenes on a hot summer day.

Tucked away beyond the arbor lies another lovely garden room, this one bounded on three sides by walls of white lattice and birches. The lattice establishes an airy, country atmosphere while providing privacy, a rare combination in the middle of

Gwen and John Burgee's two-story penthouse comprises several garden rooms that seem far removed from the cares of city life. On the lower floor (opposite), a translucent awning bathes the breakfast table in a warm golden glow. The second story (below) has an intimate garden whose walls of lattice and white birches establish an atmosphere at once airy, pastoral, and private—a rare combination in the middle of Manhattan.

151

Manhattan. Here in this outdoor room, the annoying sounds of city traffic are obscured by the sound of birch leaves rustling in the wind. Red roses climbing up the lattice walls fill the air with their rich perfume. The view through the arbor toward the lily pond creates the illusion of expansive space. With its white wrought iron furniture, this becomes a romantic retreat.

Like the Burgee garden, a penthouse garden overlooking Madison Avenue was also designed to provide a great variety of garden experiences. Here, however, the connecting element is evergreen shrubs and the variety is provided by the change in additional deciduous plant materials. Whereas at the Burgee garden each garden space was clearly defined, in this one natural-wood planters continue around corners without interruption.

With great care, the owner of this marvelous penthouse terrace has surrounded his outdoor entertaining areas with layers of mugo pine, bird's-nest spruce, juniper, and a wide variety of chamaecyparis. Ivy abounds, veiling the large wooden containers. From within the refreshing shelter of the large awning, one's view is directed toward masses of evergreen shrubs, flowering crabapples, and cherry trees. The Brutalist angles of the Whitney Museum, across the street, are barely visible and one

is totally unaware of Madison Avenue far below.

A tour of this terrace is like a walk through a compact country estate. Passing through an orchard of crabapples—our host likes to boast about his native Madison Avenue crabapple jelly—the guest then rounds the corner from the sitting area to enter a lush green hallway. Climbing roses, ivy, and pyracantha grace the walls; andromeda, euonymous, arborvitae, and yew line the path. Tucked into the ivy plantings is an intriguing collection of found objects including shells and black "lucky" stones, smoothed by ocean waves. Beyond a natural arch of forsythia is a solitary park bench, placed before a wrought iron fence that has become totally engulfed by clematis and silverlace vine. All around are exquisite specimen Japanese maple trees.

Wood decking is useful in distributing additional loads on rooftops that originally may not have been designed to accommodate a garden; it also protects the waterproof surface of the roof. Up on a decked roof in the middle of New York City's SoHo—with 125 water towers within view—everything is casual, colorful, and fun. Flags ruffle in the wind, pots of festive petunias, black-eyed Susans, herbs, and

Opposite and below: *Even the most incapacious of penthouse spaces can bring the pleasures of the country to the city. The owner of this Park Avenue penthouse raises the American flag first thing every morning then, on warm summer days, moves around the corner to enjoy breakfast.*

ing table. A country gate opens to an intimate sitting area, perfect for reading alone or a lunch for two.

This is a rooftop garden that expands with the party. Everything is movable: the wooden planters are lightweight and can easily be shifted when additional furniture and potted plants are moved outside for special occasions. Each year, this spacious rooftop easily accommodates fifty or more people who gather to celebrate the arrival of summer. As the sky fills with spectacular bands of color, the guests raise a glass to friendship and the summer months to follow.

and many nearby rooftop gardens within earshot, this decked roof in the middle of New York's SoHo is part of a neighborhood in the sky. Here, everything is casual: planters and furniture are lightweight and movable, making them easy to change with the season or the occasion.

As Water Flows

Water refreshes. The sight of it is intriguing; its pervasive melodies can filter through gardens to establish auditory buffers that protect those within hearing from the often annoying noise of surrounding activities. It may be natural to the site or introduced by man, but water—more than any other element—brings the requisite qualities for unifying a garden, bestowing both focus and purpose. Whether in an intimate garden, an entrance courtyard, or a large backyard, water is the lifeblood and is extremely useful in establishing a garden's tone.

Fountains, pools, streams—the slightest sound of moving water draws people into its presence, as does the reflection in a sheet of still water. As it is so important, water must be incorporated into the design of a garden with great care.

Scale and proportion are critical elements in the successful integration of water into the landscape. Along the coast of Rhode Island, Lloyd Lawton designed a wonderful garden in which water is incorporated on two scales: the terrace garden, perched atop a rocky promontory, captures dramatic views of the ocean from the surrounding scenery, while the intimate garden features a lily pond.

As a grand painting dominates a living room, the view of the ever-changing light on the rocky shore and the seemingly endless expanse of ocean captivates all visitors to this terrace. The garden has been sensitively planted with perennials, shrubs, and a few carefully chosen trees to take full advantage of this spectacular view. The focus toward the ocean is manipulated by a dramatically pruned Russian olive and masses of bayberry. Perennials in soft silvers, whites, pinks, and blues stand out against the green shrub border, providing a delicate foreground.

Continually serenaded by the gentle sound of trickling water, the guest is enticed down through a lovely, flower-filled rock garden to the intimate garden, where a small pool is nestled into the rocks and surrounded by masses of perennials that are protected from the often harsh sea breeze. Pink geraniums and white baby'sbreath, orange and yellow daylilies, blue platycodon, lady's-mantle, heather, juniper, and a dwarf blue spruce all conspire to create a natural setting for the pool that is rich in both color and texture.

The great variety of sounds created by the different sources of water in this garden provides continuous pleasure while contributing to the overall ambience. Here, the sounds have been orchestrated. The delicate trickle of water flowing into the pool complements the soothing but sometimes monotonous ocean waves, enveloping the garden in constantly changing sound.

On a smaller scale, the sound of water establishes a soothing ambience for a terrace garden tucked away behind an unprepossessing house in North Seattle. With the imaginative addition of a waterfall, Steve Lindjord has created an urban oasis, an island of brick surrounded by steep, lushly planted slopes and the magic of water. A series of cascades, emerging from a source hidden high among rustling pampas grass, flows down the ivy-covered embankment and ends in a lovely, small lily pond set into the slope three feet above the terrace. Sitting at the table with the water at eye level, the diner feels surrounded and soothed by the water's close proximity: the sound of the flowing water has been planned to enfold this intimate

Below: *The gentle sound of trickling water draws one along a stepping-stone path* (left) *to this lily pond* (right) *tucked into a sumptuous array of perennials in a coastal Rhode Island garden. In another lily pool* (opposite), *one designed by Alice Recknagel Ireys for an East Hampton garden, goldfish, water lilies, and pickerel rush highlight the water's surface, buddleia bobs in the breeze at water's edge, and butterflies flutter all around.*

neighbors.

In a large enclosed garden in the Napa Valley, cascading water commands the view and focuses attention, both visually and with its luxuriant, all-encompassing sounds. Here, landscape architect Jack Chandler has designed a fountain wall for drama as well as privacy at the home of Jake and Dolores Cakebread, owners of the Cakebread Wine Cellars.

Their garden plays several roles. The terrace is comfortable for entertaining just a few friends, and with its adjacent lawn, it also accommodates large parties and wine tastings during harvest time. Combining high fences, trees, and stone walls, Chandler has enclosed the terrace and successfully separated the garden from the great activity of the adjacent main road and the Cakebread Wine Cellars. Surrounded by beds of colorful flowers, overhanging pecan trees, and the magnificent fountain, the garden takes on an inward focus.

With the fountain wall, Chandler has created a view that sets the tone for the whole garden. All are attracted to the play of the brilliant California sunlight on the water as it flows from its source at the top of the wall to the pool below. The water shimmers as it falls first from chutes in ribbons of silver, then in wider sheets over the steps of dark adobe pavers, ending in a narrow pool. An impressive terra cotta pot of pa-

Chandler is the centerpiece of Jake and Dolores Cakebread's garden in California's Napa Valley.

160

accent against the warm brown of the Napa stone wall. The fountain commands the view throughout the garden while obscuring the noise of passing traffic; it relaxes vineyard guests, permitting them to settle back and enjoy the flavors of the wines to their fullest.

The sound of water is also used to great effect in formal gardens. Like the fountain wall, an Italian fountain designed by Emmet L. Wemple & Associates rises high above a multitude of magnificent hybrid roses, thus dominating a Los Angeles garden comprising several entertaining areas. Separated by low hedges and walls, the fountain, with its impressive height and many levels of flowing water, establishes a visual and aural link between the various garden spaces. It lures the visitor along the gravel paths of the rose garden to the fish pool at its base, and the sound of splashing water combined with the fragrance of roses is a heady experience.

At Belle Vista in Southport, Connecticut, fountains are included to provide a spectacular accent for a formal swimming pool, the centerpiece of the garden.

Set in its own garden room, the dramatic elliptical pool is surrounded by a wide carpet of bright-green lawn and an eight-foot-high natural wall of hemlocks. Entering from the house, the visitor gravi-

ambience while they mask sounds from nearby neighbors.

Opposite: *Rising elegantly above an exquisite collection of roses, an Italian fountain dominates the view from all corners of this Los Angeles garden designed by Emmet L. Wemple & Associates.*

Alice Pickman has incorporated a "diving rock" at the edge of this pool in Brookline, Massachusetts (below), where it blends beautifully with the impressive formation of rocks on the hillside.

Manship. Framed by an opening in the hedge and the rhododendron park beyond, the gushing jets of water splash into the pool. Black, with charcoal tile trim and bluestone coping, the pool reflects the sky and trees, tying the pool into the garden as a whole.

While large enough to accommodate sit-down dinners for over one hundred, this outdoor room is also very personal and private. During the day it is a favorite place to read in the sun or to cool off after a game of tennis.

Swimming pools have become a versatile element in the landscape. In the past, they conjured up images of flat, bright-blue rectangles surrounded by concrete. Today they are designed with such attention to detail that they serve as ornaments in the landscape as well as centers for outdoor gatherings, and while they are still the spot for a refreshing dip, they are also much more.

A waterfall flowing over a dragonlike formation of rocks is the water source for a swimming pool in Brookline, Massachusetts. Designed by landscape architect Alice Pickman, the pool is set into a steep hillside adjacent to an old apple orchard. The waterfall, composed of rocks from neglected stone walls on the property, begins

near Santa Barbara, landscape architect Isabelle C. Greene has related the house's clean lines to the huge expanse of the Pacific Ocean below by creating a landscape of pools and boulders that seem to tumble down the hillside.

at the foot of Swiss stone pines and follows the slope. The owners like to think of it as being "like the water coming off Mt. Washington," the pines suggestive of the mountain's peak.

Hidden behind a high fence on one side, and far uphill from the house on another, the pool is at the center of a secret garden, set far apart from the daily activities of the surrounding farm. From the house, only a stone wall topped by a colorful perennial border is visible.

This is most of all a fun garden, full of fantasy and color. A pavilion evokes mysterious images while providing shade from the hot midday sun. The large rock, surrounded by an exuberant concatenation of flowers, is actually the "diving board." A grassy bank has been graded at just the right angle for sunbathing. This pool garden is a favorite place for adults to relax and for children to play without fear of annoying their parents. Parties around the pool on warm summer nights, lit entirely by torchlight, lift guests out of the New England setting and send them to the realms at the far reaches of their imaginations.

In contrast to this New England garden, a swimming pool in Santa Barbara, California, was designed as an integral element in the landscape and a focus from the house. When standing on the terrace of this home, perched high on a bluff, an intriguing

Guests to this pool garden on the shores of Seattle's Lake Washington (opposite) *can arrive by car, boat, or seaplane!*

Shade from these stunning poolside pavilions designed by Jack Chandler (below) *makes this an ideal setting for casual wine tastings at Gary Ramona's Napa Valley home.*

169

endless expanse of the Pacific Ocean one hundred feet below. Huge boulders seem to tumble down the hillside until they come to rest at the edge of a swimming pool. Sensuous mounds of soft, green, drought-tolerant plants gently roll down to the edge of the relatively flat lawn. The landscape architect, Isabelle C. Greene, has designed a fascinating garden that incorporates the suggestion of flowing water. Ironically, actual running water here could cause a landslide and thus destroy this environmentally sensitive setting.

The five different bodies of water that follow one another as they descend from the house are all interrelated within this one garden—a reflecting pool, spa, lily pond, swimming pool, and the ocean itself. Designed on many levels, each of the pools is surrounded by its own terrace and fulfills a different social function.

Set into the terrace adjacent to the house's living room, the reflecting pool, with its mirror image of the surrounding trees and sky and its sensuous curve, pushes the garden into the entertaining area. Wide timber steps seem to flow like a "streambed" from the living room terrace to a small terrace with a pondlike spa, midway down the slope. Irregularly shaped, with large local stones forming the sides and steps down into the water, the spa

strong geometric lines of this pool and terrace designed by Jack Chandler (below and opposite). Water spouts, terra cotta olive jars, and the wooden pergola turn the pool into an exotic counterpoint to the surrounding Napa Valley vineyards.

jasmine, and agapanthus grow right up to the rocky edge, surrounding all those within the spa with a profusion of colors and fragrances. Obscured by larger boulders and mounding shrubs, the spa is visible only from the upper terrace and walkway, not from the swimming pool and lawn below.

As the "streambed" continues its course down the hill, it jogs around boulders and masses of shrubs before culminating in a lily pond, which from above appears to be part of the swimming pool. Boulders from the "streambed" traverse the pool, shattering its rectilinear lines. Water lilies and pickerel rush insert a natural element and attract visitors to the water's edge. With the addition of the lily pond, the swimming pool becomes multifunctional. Not only is it an excellent space for swimming and entertaining, but also a soothing one for solitary contemplation.

A swimming pool might also come as a surprise. At Lakewold, in Tacoma, Washington, a pool designed by Thomas D. Church (one of the foremost landscape architects of the twentieth century) is set out of view in its own alcove. A picturesque teahouse at the end of a long brick path beckons to the visitor to venture out into the magical garden. Walking first past parterre beds with topiary birds, then past

... Mediterranean-style pool, in a Los Angeles garden designed by Walter Heideman of Emmet L. Wemple & Associates.

172

stands of native Douglas fir, the explorer then finds that the path widens into beautifully manicured, open lawns, the stage for the delightful teahouse. At this point, looking to the left, one is greeted with a view of the exquisite quatrefoil swimming pool sparkling like a jewel. To the right, Mt. Rainier rises majestically within the frame of native firs. In this spectacular setting the teahouse and swimming pool provide ideal circumstances for relaxation after a round of golf, dinner parties under the stars, and even an afternoon concert.

The teahouse, one of the original structures on this historic estate, effectively disguises a kitchen to one side and a dressing room (hidden behind lattice walls) to the other. Covered with the sweet-smelling, old-fashioned musk rose "Kathleen," surrounded by white rhododendrons and azaleas, and filled with planters and hanging baskets of pink fuchsia, the teahouse enfolds guests completely in a garden. With its ceiling and walls of flowers, it is an intimate retreat as well as the focus of the garden.

When Church designed the swimming pool, he chose the shape to reflect the quatrefoil pattern of the teahouse floor. Conceived as both garden ornament and functioning pool, it is on axis with a Queen Anne sundial and Mt. Rainier—a juxtaposition that imposes a perfect harmony upon the garden and its spectacular setting.

Conceived by Thomas D. Church as a garden ornament, the quatrefoil swimming pool at Lakewold in Tacoma, Washington is on axis with Mt. Rainier. Although the pool appears to be deceptively small in this grand setting, its forty-foot diameter makes it quite functional—just right for swimming laps.

Walled perennial gardens are customarily built around carpets of green lawn or decorative lily ponds and fish pools. At one Connecticut home, a swimming pool in the perennial garden is also a reflecting pool and the center for many gatherings. Whereas the pool at Lakewold was set off to one side of the garden's central axis, here the pool *is* the garden's axis. A lovely focus from the screened-in porch and kitchen terrace, it also functions as a foreground element, directing the eye to Long Island Sound in the distance.

This exquisite pool is as refreshing to look at as it is to swim in. Surrounded by myriad peonies, roses, and delphiniums in June, the perennial border is planted to supply continuous color throughout the summer. An exquisite collection of antique outdoor furniture arranged in casual groupings sets the tone. This is a garden to please all the senses. The swimming pool refreshes while the abundance of flowers fills the air with sweet aromas and thrills the eye with its colorful profusion.

Due to the increased concern with pool safety, fencing has become an important factor in their design. In creating a separate garden for the pool, the fencing can easily be incorporated into the overall plan. With the imaginative use of reinforced plexiglass, fine copper screening, wood fencing, and hedges, swimming pools can meet

This swimming pool in Westport, Connecticut was originally set apart from the perennial garden and was surrounded only by a carpet of lawn. The addition of a stone wall and herbaceous border better defined the pool area and established an intimate garden space that is perfect for entertaining.

an integral part of the garden design, not in competition with it.

The surround for a mosaic-tiled pool in Los Angeles is a bougainvillaea-covered wall, which enhances the Mediterranean ambience while it separates it from an adjacent lawn terrace. A reinforced-plexiglass fence designed by Dutch Strawbridge for his pool near Newport, Rhode Island, at once encloses the pool area and incorporates the view of adjacent golden fields as an integral part of the garden. A pool in East Hampton on Long Island is surrounded by a massive privet hedge, pine trees, and a berm heavily planted with daylilies. These evergreen walls disguise the fence at the same time that they provide much-desired privacy from nearby neighbors. With the view directed out toward the ocean, this pool garden is also a lovely space for casual entertaining.

To create a pine-enclosed room for a pool on the coast of southern New England, the owners blasted a large, gently curving bowl out of a granite peninsula. The pool and surrounding terrace are set many feet below the existing grade, protected from the often cold ocean breezes. Orange daylilies and low-growing junipers encasing the sloping walls lead the eye up into the depths of the enclosing black pines

ming pool of the adjacent rose garden and fields, Dutch Strawbridge designed a fence of reinforced plexiglass panels. Another approach to minimizing the presence of pool fencing is to hide it. The enclosure for a pool that was blasted out of a granite peninsula (opposite) *is hidden among the black pines at the top of the embracing slope.*

world apart. Convenient to the house, with dressing rooms and a shaded deck, this pool room is also designed to accommodate large parties.

For a pool garden in Lincoln, Massachusetts, Alice Pickman borrowed fine proportion, clean lines, and meticulous attention to detail from Japanese design. Working closely with the owner, she created a garden with a Japanese feel and an all-American purpose: it is an exquisite garden room in which to swim and play or relax and contemplate.

Enclosed on all sides, this separate garden room was designed as a totally private world. On the two sides facing the house and entrance drive, the garden is completely hidden from view by a high wall and pool house. A low retaining wall and a transparent fence of copper screening define the remaining two sides while allowing the surrounding New England landscape to become an integral part of the garden visually.

In this garden, Mrs. Pickman has successfully brought harmony to an outdoor swimming "room." Entering through the massive gateway, one is immediately impressed by the close attention paid to detail and function. The doors are handcrafted from vertical-grain fir, with detailing of

moved all her roses to "The Hospital Bed," a protected spot down the hill. When this photograph was taken, thirty-two years later, Seattle was once again experiencing unfortunate weather—a drought. This time the lovely pond came to the rescue, providing water for the plant infirmary. Once again the roses were saved.

as a pool for all ages. A stone footbridge crossing a narrow alcove in the pool performs another aesthetic function by obscuring a submerged net that separates the children's splash pool from the deeper water. Two sculptural rocks are sensitively positioned so that one functions as a diving board and the other as a handhold at the top of the stone steps descending into the pool. As a chrome ladder would have been a glaring intrusion into this tranquil environment, the pool ladder was wrapped in teak and bronze wire. With a "mutual respect for elegant yet functional designs," Mrs. Pickman and the owner have created a very special garden room that is the owner's world apart.

Although water is considered by many to be an essential element in a garden, it is not always natural to the environment. For the owner of a stark, geometric home in Montecito, California, Isabelle C. Greene designed an intriguing garden that provides the illusion of water flowing through it. Inspired by images of rice patties and farmland as seen from the air, the garden's beds are shaped into irregular fields of color and terraced into the hillside. While the plant materials for the entire garden were se-

*stark geometry of a Montecito home. Inspired by aerial views of rice paddies, terraces are stepped down the south-facing slope. To the west (be-*low left), *the constantly changing beds include English lavender, roses interplanted with chives, and a triangle of meadow flowers; cordoned apple trees form an elegant fence, and a copper arbor makes a striking accent* (below right). *To the east* (opposite and overleaf), *the garden was designed to provide the illusion of water flowing from terrace to terrace. Complemented by a palette of drought-tolerant plants, slate slabs that glisten in the brilliant California sunlight were employed to simulate streams cutting through the landscape.*

uneven surface of slate slabs reflects the
harsh California sunlight as if from the
surface of flowing water. As this simulated
"stream" cuts a course away from the house
through terraces of silvery *Cerastium tomen-
tosum* and *Senecio serpens*, it meanders around
agaves, aloes, and yuccas, which resemble
boulders in the stream. Further down, the
"stream" divides to become a "delta," its
fingers extending to a field of brilliant red
Crassula falcata and the edge of a desertlike
terrace, or as Greene says, "to the end of the
fantasy."

Landscape architect Alice Ireys has also
used water to bring fantasy and enchantment to a hillside garden. In East
Hampton she has designed an extensive
waterfall where before there was only a
steeply sloping hillside. This waterfall
joins the house and brick dining terrace,
perched high above, with the garden and
swimming pool below, adding a whole
new dimension to the owners' use of the
garden.

Appearing, as if by magic, from a natural grouping of large rocks, the waterfall is
designed as a continuous series of visual
and auditory experiences. It enriches the
garden as it flows down the hillside, establishing a link between the terrace and

house above and the gardens below. The waterfall bathes the house and gardens with its soothing sound, thereby obscuring the noise of cars passing nearby. As its flow can easily be adjusted, it is possible to summon up just the right ambient-sound level for any occasion.

Descending the staircase that follows the course of the waterfall, the guest becomes aware of the subtle changes in the sonorities emanating from the water as it flows over small stones, then larger ones in turn, on its journey to the pool below. Midway down the hillside, the waterfall levels off slightly and the steps are interrupted by a gently sloping ramp. The change of pace enhances the experience, making one aware of the profusion of woodland flowers, ferns, and irises that contrast with the solidity and hardness of the boulders, setting a wonderfully wild tone at the water's edge. At the bottom of the hill, a bridge crossing the brook provides the perfect spot from which to look up and experience the full effect of the descending water surrounded by the lush green foliage or, on the other side, to enjoy the lovely lily pond, filled with colorful koi, created at the cascade's endpoint.

Hidden among masses of white buddleia bobbing in the breeze, the lily pond is alive and romantic, its surface constantly changing as it reflects the surrounding garden and sky above. Large orange and

Pages 183–185: *With the use of recirculating pumps, landscape architect Alice Recknagel Ireys has created a natural-looking stream that flows over a series of large stones and small waterfalls on its sixty-foot journey from the house above to the fish pool at its terminus. This waterfall has bestowed a touch of fantasy on what before had been simply a steep hillside in East Hampton.*

fill the air.

Continuing across the bridge and down the steps, the visitor arrives in an exquisite garden with perennial beds to the left, a swimming pool to the right, and a wisteria-covered gazebo to the side, with a picturesque vegetable garden and orchard in the distance.

One of the owner's most memorable parties was held in this lower garden—an afternoon tea. The lawn was dotted with small tables dressed with green tablecloths and summer flowers from the garden. As guests descended the staircase they were refreshed by the waterfall then enchanted by the vision of the garden party as it unfolded before them, their hostess awaiting them at the foot of the stairs with tea and glasses of chilled champagne.

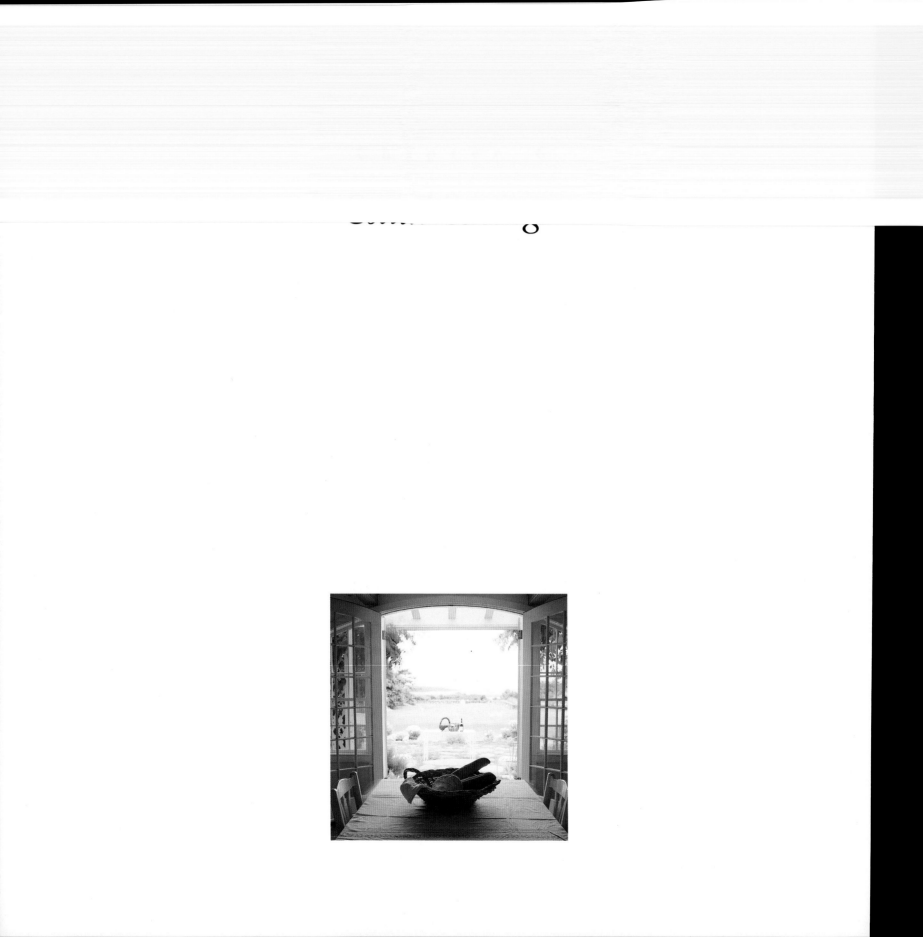

Setting a scene in which guests immediately feel at ease is one of the most important ingredients in successful entertaining. Comfort is also key and many of the same elements considered when furnishing a living or dining room must be taken into account when appointing an outdoor space for living and entertaining.

It is wise always to have at least one outdoor space set up so that it can be used for entertaining throughout the season. In the case of John Saladino's garden, this is an elegant gravel terrace adjacent to the house. Organized into sitting and dining areas, furnished with wrought iron tables and chairs, and shaded by large, white, Italian-market umbrellas, it is delightful from spring into fall.

Climate is the most influential consideration when furnishing a comfortable outdoor space for entertaining. Protection from the sun is essential, especially in warm climates. When incorporated into the total design of a garden room, shading devices—pergolas, awnings, arbors, trees, umbrellas—help to create atmosphere as well as the necessary shade. The embrace of a wisteria arbor often encourages intimate conversation while the cool shade provides a refreshing escape from the hot summer sun. A feathery tree such as a honey locust provides delicate, dappled shade without inhibiting the flow of cooling summer breezes. Awnings and umbrellas are especially flexible additions to a terrace design. Awnings can be rolled up to allow bright sunlight into the house, while umbrellas can be folded up and removed altogether.

Lisa Stamm has complemented her gazebo with a number of white canvas umbrellas on wheels to provide shade beside her elegant swimming pool on Shelter Island. For her, the greatest advantage to including the umbrellas lies in their portability, which affords greater control of the area to be shaded. However, she also loves the way they glow in the sunlight against the sea of pink roses surrounding the pool. White Italian-market umbrellas not only add a festive flair but also provide a luminous focal point when viewed from a distance.

Color, versatility, and durability are major considerations when selecting an umbrella or awning. Wind can tear fragile fabrics while sun, salt air, and pollution all accelerate their bleaching and disintegration. Synthetic fabrics, such as acrylics, tend to be more resistant to fading and mildew. But the soft, bleached look of canvas is often more suitable to the garden setting.

When deciding on a color, be sure to give careful thought to the color that light filtering through the umbrella or awning will bestow. People and food should look appealing in the shadow. A translucent yellow awning bathes the area beneath it in a warm, golden glow. If only a green awning or umbrella will do, it should be made of an opaque material, as green light is not flattering to the complexion.

Umbrellas bring to mind visions of parasols in Impressionist paintings, or colorful beach umbrellas glowing in the brilliant summer light. Today, however, an increasing number of manufacturers are offering square and rectangular umbrellas as well as those in the more traditional round shape, making it possible to select the exact size and shape for each purpose.

As umbrellas increase in size, however, structure and stability become even more important, especially in windy locations. The umbrella should be sturdy with smooth, easily maneuvered mechanisms for raising and lowering. For people who

The color of the light that will filter through an umbrella or awning is an important consideration in its selection. Here, the terrace adjacent to the loggia of John Saladino's Connecticut home is endowed with a refreshing, cool light from its awning.

are best. Nothing ruins an appetite faster than pulling up to a table for lunch and stubbing a toe on a bulky, metal umbrella stand.

An inventive solution to the umbrella-stand dilemma is to eliminate it altogether. Sleeves, similar in concept to the cups used in golf greens, can be set right into the terrace. One friend has installed such sleeves in the terrace around her pool; when they're not in use, she covers them with metal caps. These sleeves provide the flexibility that allows her to put all the umbrellas up at one end of the pool or to create shaded sitting areas at both ends.

Comfortable furniture will draw people into the garden. Just as it does in the living room of one's home, furniture completes the outdoor entertaining area. And, like a living room, the garden ideally should accommodate several sitting areas. A terrace in Seattle functions beautifully, organized into two portions for sitting, with an adjacent dining area. It is perfect for entertaining up to twenty-four guests at a time.

Arranging the furniture in casual groups encourages people to sit, talk, and have a good time. Chairs positioned to take ad-

Stands for large umbrellas are often weighted for stability. Lisa Stamm installed her umbrellas on wheeled, wooden platforms so they can be easily moved with the arc of the sun.

guests to appr~

Small side tables arranged to be within easy reach for drinks, books, and food permit the guests' relaxation and enjoyment without the challenge of balancing everything at once on a lap or in hand. Comfortable chaises, or chairs with ottomans, set off to the side are favorite places for reading and relaxing. Ottomans can always double as tables or extra seats during large parties, and some furniture manufacturers offer plastic trays that fit securely on top. Lightweight, movable chairs are convenient for guests to pull up to join in conversations. Seating walls and built-in benches provide welcome additional seating especially in small gardens. It is, however, very difficult to carry on a conversation with several people if everyone is sitting in a straight line. To encourage conversation, permanent benches should be designed as alcoves or with angles whenever possible.

The most successful terraces are those designed to accommodate a variety of furniture arrangements, depending on the size of the party. Dawn Mello's Park Avenue terrace is normally set up for six-person dinners. With the addition of two forty-eight-inch, round tables for four, it easily accommodates a dinner for twelve. To determine the minimum number of chairs to provide in the sitting area, first consider the number you most often serve at the

Italian-market umbrellas add a festive accent to both informal garden spaces and formal terraces.

dining room table; the number of chairs in the sitting area should correspond. For instance, if your dining room table seats twelve and you enjoy serving drinks on the terrace before moving inside for dinner, be sure the terrace is designed to seat all twelve guests comfortably.

Designing a garden to include formal as well as informal dining areas allows for greater variety in entertaining. A dining area adjacent to the house is excellent for formal entertaining, while a poolside table is perfect for lunch and more casual dining. Picnic tables are easily moved and can be dressed up with tablecloths for special occasions. If you have space for only one table, it is important that it be versatile. Those that seat either four or six comfortably are preferable. While tables of wrought iron and glass are always formal, the clean, modern lines of aluminum or resin furniture span all styles. With so many different types of outdoor furniture from which to choose, it is best to begin by determining which style complements the character of both the house and the garden. Chairs that are comfortable with or without cushions are ideal.

Choosing the fabric for a garden room is just as important a decision as choosing the fabric for a living room. The right fabric both enhances the garden and completes its desired look. Bright colors, solids, wild floral patterns, stripes, and pastels all can

Pergolas, being open to the sky, can bring the visual excitement of distinct shadows to garden spaces (below), *and provide an elegant transition between house and garden* (opposite).

have a place in the garden, but their selection must be thoughtfully considered for each particular situation. In a confined area, a multicolored fabric will attract too much attention, making the space appear smaller, perhaps claustrophobic; solid coverings are much more suitable to a small terrace. When choosing the fabric for dining chairs, opt for colors that complement the place settings and the flowers in adjacent herbaceous borders. Orange cushions can be jarring if everything else is in tones of pink. In rainy climates, cushions that dry quickly and do not retain moisture relieve their owner of the tiresome job of taking the cushions in after each use. If fragile fabrics are necessary to create the desired ambience, provide adequate storage for the cushions within close proximity to the terrace.

Furniture by the pool should be comfortable, easily movable, and versatile. As it is probably going to remain outside for an entire season, the furniture should be resistant both to rust and the sun's destructive ultraviolet rays, and should be easily washable as well. In warm climates, it is especially important that all pool furniture remain cool to the touch, even at high noon, as most people using it will be wearing bathing suits. Pool furniture with mesh seats breathes and therefore remains cool. Wet bathing suits can also play havoc with cushions. Check all fabrics for color-

Lightweight furniture allows for greater versatility in the garden. It can be moved easily to take advantage of views, sun or shade, and cooling summer breezes.

fastness and resistance to mildew. Stylish wooden chaises are extremely versatile for poolside as they double elegantly as low tables when in their fully horizontal position, their cushions removed. Most aluminum and wrought iron furniture can be ordered with unbreakable plastic table tops; it is unwise to use glass next to a pool. In climates with severe winters, it will be necessary to store outdoor furniture. If space is a problem, choose furniture made of lightweight coated aluminum or resin that stacks easily.

When setting the lawn terrace, lightweight furniture is always best. Not only is it necessary to move it for lawn maintenance but, as Diane McGuire succinctly puts it: "Garden furniture should always be mobile because there are times when you want sun and times when you want shade. Times when you want to be in the wind and times when you don't. Heavy benches are best used as a focal point or terminus." One hostess who was very meticulous in positioning her lawn furniture set small markers of flagstone in the lawn. When the gardener removed the furniture to mow the lawn he was always able to return each piece to its designated position.

For special events, however, furniture need not be lightweight—or traditional. One friend, when faced with the prospect of seating twenty, used bales of hay for table and chairs. He stacked the bales two high

A pair of chaises set to the side of a Seattle, Washington terrace provide a comfortable place to read and relax (below), *while a heavy English teak bench functions as a focal point at the end of a Shelter Island swimming pool* (opposite). *Those beside a pool in Portland, Oregon can elegantly double as tables* (overleaf).

and three wide for the table. The continuous benches on either side had seats one bale high with two-bale backs. Covered with Oriental rugs, the hay-bale benches were soft and luxurious, encouraging all to relax and have a good time. The tablecloths of India-print fabric, bud vases with cheerful annuals, and candles in steady stands transformed the hay bales, completing this imaginative, magical setting. To set a Southwestern tone, Navajo rugs could be used in combination with sunflowers, zinnias, and black-eyed Susans. And the soft pastel colors of dhurries could be used in harmony with the many flowers of July—roses, phlox, scabiosa, and cosmos. For the more ambitious, heavy fabrics such as canvas or a painter's dropcloth could even be handpainted.

Benches command a view. Traditionally made of wood, stone, or cast iron, benches act as havens, luring guests to secluded corners with invitations to sit, relax, and contemplate the lovely surroundings. A bench curved to fit snugly up against a garden wall or around the base of a tree provides a special vantage point from which to enjoy a garden. A rustic wood bench fades beautifully into the wild tangle of a woodland setting, while a classic, weathered teak bench nestles harmoniously among the colorful masses of flowers in a cottage garden. The sleek lines of a smooth mahogany bench painted white are remi-

niscent of summer and conjure up images of white furniture sitting elegantly on a brilliant green lawn overlooking a rocky seacoast. Ornate cast iron benches, popular at the turn of the century, are often designed with such botanical patterns as intertwining grape vines, branches, or intricate ferns. They add a special flair to rose gardens as decorative focal points and contribute to the romantic ambience in intimate garden rooms.

Garden ornaments like urns, planters, and hanging baskets are excellent accents on terraces in the city as well as the country. The plantings add a splash of color, which can be changed for special occasions or with the seasons of the year. Planters effectively define space by breaking up large expanses of terrace. On Dawn Mello's penthouse terrace, planters topped with cone-shaped trelliswork and clematis set the sitting area apart from the dining area. Richard Anderson is constantly on the lookout for interesting ornaments for his Albany, New York, garden. Urns of varying shapes and sizes, combined with intricate architectural pediments, establish an historical tone in his Italian garden. Birdbaths, feeders, and houses attract additional movement and life to the garden and often provide the focus. Ornamental faucets, perhaps in the shape of quails or sparrows, can be useful in concealing water sources. Garden ornaments should be selected with

Treillage and garden ornaments add a flair to urban and rural terraces alike. Lattice brings the country to Dawn Mellow's penthouse terrace in New York (below) *and provides enclosure for the rose-covered teahouse at Lakewold in Tacoma, Washington* (opposite).

care to ensure that they contribute to, and don't detract from, a garden's special personality.

Every outdoor space for living and entertaining develops its own character. Many draw upon the garden itself and its established aura as a wonderful source of inspiration for creating memorable social settings. The seasonal changes of color—or its subtle transitions in a perennial border or a flowering tree in full bloom—offer departure points from which to develop the right ambience for each occasion.

In the case of a garden with many outdoor rooms, such as John Saladino's, it is a particular garden that determines the setting. As Saladino proudly explains, "My garden is like a series of theatres. As the curtain comes down on one stage, it rises on another." Saladino takes great pleasure in changing the setting for his outdoor parties as each garden reaches its zenith. Serving cocktails in the vegetable garden when the vegetables are beautifully ripe is a wonderful, refreshing way to begin an evening. Here the garden both sets the tone and provides the hors d'oeuvre. A bowl brimming with fresh-picked cherry tomatoes awaits under the watchful eyes of towering topiary birds. Served on a mound of crushed ice, surrounded with bowls of vodka, curry, and salt in which to dip them, the tomatoes look cool and appetiz-

When the tomatoes are ripe and the lettuce forms beautiful full heads, the vegetable garden under the watchful eyes of John Saladino's topiary birds (opposite) becomes a favorite place to entertain. Another lovely summer setting lies within the embrace of espaliered apple trees and roses in a Westport, Connecticut garden (below).

ing, setting a festive tone for the evening to follow. In June, when the lavender and white violets are in bloom, the horseshoe garden is a favorite place for luncheons and formal teas.

The predominant color of a garden in bloom is a lovely departure point for planning any social event. Table settings can coordinate with the flowers—pink for the cherry tree, lavender for the lilacs, blue for cornflowers or delphinium, orange and yellow for California poppies. The results can be equally inviting, however, if a single color scheme is carried throughout, in the furnishings as well as the table settings: a Seattle hostess dresses her table with green and white linens and china, which she has collected from all over the world; Dawn Mello sets a stylish black and white table, often incorporating topiary herbs and pots of flowers as colorful accents.

The greatest fun can come from planning the table setting for special occasions. Don't be afraid to experiment. Look to the garden for inspiration. To create the centerpiece for one July luncheon on the terrace, I filled a large bowl with four perfect heads of green, saladbowl leaf lettuce. Next I tucked bright-orange nasturtiums in among the leaves. Cobalt-blue glass plates and highball glasses complemented the nasturtiums, enhancing their glow in the brilliant summer sunlight. Napkins from

Opposite: Saturday afternoon perfection in Stowe, Vermont. Guests arrive via buckboard pulled by Bob and Jerry to be greeted by George the billygoat and a devilishly handsome Polish rooster. From this niche carved out of the expansive fields, they savor the view toward the Green Mountains.

Topped with a festive tequila sunrise can, a bright-red tractor evokes images of the countryside even though it's in Westport, Connecticut (below left). A wine press adds an appropriate touch to a garden in the midst of the Mondavi Vineyards in Napa Valley (below right).

Provence added a fresh, colorful accent to the casual setting.

When planning a table setting that depends on color coordination for success, it is important to give careful thought to the surface of the outdoor dining table. Weathered teak or white resin table tops are excellent for luncheons by the pool, but for candlelit dinners, tablecloths add a special touch, transforming the garden with their soft texture and flowing line.

A dinner for one hundred and twenty automatically takes on a formal tone due to its grand size. To set a more casual tone, one hostess handpainted tablecloths in Pointillist-inspired pastel patterns. In the center of each round table for six, she placed bread fashioned into baskets, and several small vases of roses from her garden. Bathed in soft light reflected from the swimming pool, the garden setting appeared intimate and romantic within its walls of eight-foot-high hemlocks.

Don't be afraid to bring the good glasses outdoors, especially when serving champagne or fine wine. Excellent stemware adds an elegance to a setting while the enjoyment of the wine is enhanced by the feel of the flute or goblet to the hand and against the lips. Plastic glasses often have rough edges and can contribute a flavor that interferes with the wine. When selecting glassware for outdoor entertaining, be sure that the pieces have weighted bottoms

On hot summer days, what could be more refreshing than a swim and a picnic by a lake? The rustic shelter houses a bar and the clearing by a lake deep in the woods of Vermont provides an ideal setting for entertaining. Guests arrive on horseback, by wagon, or occasionally on foot.

to prevent their blowing over in a strong wind. One should also take care that all tables are steady. When a hostess in Rhode Island entertains on her lawn terrace, everything is bright and cheerful to blend with the surrounding herbaceous border. Chilled white wine is served in extraordinary glasses handpainted with yellow, red, and blue flowers, thereby bringing the garden to the table.

For barbeques and clambakes alike, paper plates and plastic utensils often make the most sense. In these cases go all out. By their nature, these events inevitably lead to a big mess, so make it work for you. Cover the table with sheets of kraft paper and use large, striped cotton kitchen towels or bandanas as napkins. Choose colorful plates and cups to add to the festive atmosphere that always surrounds a cookout. For dessert following a lobster cookout in Rhode Island, I placed fluorescent light sticks in the center of each bowl of ice cream. The children were so thrilled with their lights, they stuck them in their sneakers and went running into the wildflower meadow to join the fireflies.

My grandmother always said, "If you're going to throw a party, make it memorable." When we visited friends in Vermont, they did just that. At noon Al pulled up to the garden gate in a buckboard wagon drawn by two impressive horses, Bob and Jerry. Our host and hostess loaded the

Three boys on dolphins—magnificent Paul Manship fountains discovered in the back room of an antique shop—provide a spectacular accent for a formal swimming pool in Southport, Connecticut. Two tables for four and another seating eight accommodate intimate lunches for two as effortlessly as luncheons for twelve or fourteen.

In a colorful perennial garden, a swimming pool is at once a reflecting pool and the center for many social gatherings. When viewed from the house, it becomes a foreground element that directs the eye to Long Island Sound in the distance.

wagon with baskets brimming over with sandwiches, fruit, wine, and cakes, then invited us to pile in. As we rode first through fields of sheep, then into the woods, we felt we were embarking on a true adventure. Before too long, we reached our destination—a beautiful, sparkling blue lake. A picnic table and bar surrounded by lush green grass and wildflowers provided a lovely social setting overlooking the lake. After an expedition in the canoe and swimming with the children, we settled down for a luncheon we will always remember.

Social gardens are celebrations of life and friendship. Visually rich and refreshing, all gardens are incomplete without people to enjoy their great pleasures. Formal or informal, large or small, social gardens bring deep joy to all who enter their realm. Sculpting a garden from the wild or creating one where before there were only rocks and rubble is a challenge for which the rewards are neverending. Sharing a garden with friends is always special, and the memories they take with them are a once-in-a-lifetime gift.

Green and white comprise the color scheme for this stunning terrace overlooking Puget Sound in Seattle. Linens and china collected by the owners during their travels around the world add a personal flair to this elegant social setting.

Resources

Directory to Designers Featured in *Social Gardens*

John Burgee Architects
885 Third Avenue
New York, NY 10022

Burton and Spitz
2324½ Michigan Avenue
Santa Monica, CA 90404
Landscape architects

Buttrick White & Burtis
475 Tenth Avenue
New York, NY 10018
Architects and interior designers

Jack Chandler & Associates
P.O. Box 2180
Yountville, CA 94599
Landscape architects

Antony Childs, Inc., ASID
1670 Wisconsin Avenue, N.W.
Washington, DC 20007
Interior designer

Barbara V. Fealy
4805 S.W. Chestnut Place
Beaverton, OR 97005
Landscape architect

Robert Genchek
29 East 22nd Street
New York, NY 10010
Architect

Christopher R. Gillespie
P.O. Box 223
Westport Point, MA 02791
Architect

Fisher Gordon Architects
1032 Wisconsin Avenue, N.W.
Washington, DC 20007

Isabelle C. Greene & Associates
34 East Sola
Santa Barbara, CA 93101
Landscape architects

Perry Guillot
55 West 75th Street
New York, NY 10023
Landscape architect

Richard Haag & Associates, Inc.
2923 Fuhrman Avenue East
Seattle, WA 98102
Landscape architects

Tim Holtschlag
P.O. Box 618
Vashon, WA 98070
Landscape designer

Alice Recknagel Ireys
45 Willow Street
Brooklyn, NY 11201
Landscape architect

Steve Lindjord
22307 Third Avenue, S.W.
Bothell, WA 98021
Landscape designer

Lippman & Mohr
5349 Newcastle Avenue #2
Encino, California 91316
Architect and contractor

Nancy McCabe
Box 447
Salisbury, CT 06068
Garden historian and designer

Diane Kostial McGuire
Barbara Harrison Watson
85 East India Row
Boston, MA 02110
Landscape architects
and horticultural consultants

Amy Meltzer
Treasured Tabletops, Inc.
(212) 535–3403
Tabletops designer

Mitchel D. Moore
701 Ocean Avenue, Suite 9
Santa Monica, CA 90402
Interior designer

Oehme, van Sweden and Associates
3109 M Street, N.W.
Washington, DC 20007
Landscape architects

Alice Pickman
213 Concord Road
Lincoln, MA 01773
Landscape architect

John F. Saladino
305 East 63rd Street
New York, NY 10021
Interior designer

Richard Schadt Associates, Inc.
224 Sixteenth Avenue
San Francisco, CA 94118
Landscape architects

Anne Smith
1225 McGilvra Boulevard East
Seattle, WA 98112
Garden designer

Lisa Stamm
67 Manantic Road
Shelter Island, NY 11965
Landscape gardener

Thomas J. Stohlman, AIA
3421½ M Street, N.W.
Washington, DC 20007
Architect

F. Raymond Strawbridge, ASID
Philip J. Wenzel
Strawbridge/Wenzel Interiors
638 West Main Road
Little Compton, RI 02837
Interior designers

Taylor Architects
522 Wilshire Boulevard, Suite J
Santa Monica, CA 90401
Architects

Hossein Vaidi Vahedi
42 Concord Square
Boston, MA 02118
Architect

Warner and Gray, Inc.
1225–A Coast Village Road
Santa Barbara, CA 93108
Architects

Emmet L. Wemple & Associates
2503 West Seventh Street
Los Angeles, CA 90057
Landscape architects

Landscape Contractors and Stonemasons

Following is a list of landscape contractors and stonemasons who work closely with some of the landscape architects featured in this book.

Acorn Landscaping
P.O. Box 6067
Santa Barbara, CA 93111
(805) 964–4900
Landscape contractors who take great care in the implementation of complex plans.

James N. Birk
Birks Company
1113 Orchard Way
Silver Spring, MD 20904
(301) 384–6174
Excels in stonework and brickwork, especially in conjunction with fountains, waterfalls, and ponds.

Harry Broderick Inc.
7327 Winnetka Avenue
Canoga Park, CA 91306
(818) 341–6323
Landscape contractor who supplies all plant materials, soils, and planting amendments; will take on responsibility for the installation of garden structures, plant materials, irrigation, and lighting.

Damas Construction
10818 East Whittier Boulevard
Whittier, CA 90606
(213) 692–0721
Landscape contractors who excel in the implementation of complex landscape plans.

Oswald Da Ros, Inc.
976 Carrillo Road
Santa Barbara, CA 93103
(805) 962–6406
A mason specializing in constructing stone walls, paving, and steps.

Gabriel Faria, Jr.
Windy Hill Nursery
Old Main Road
Little Compton, RI 02837
(401) 635–4888
Working with seaside conditions is the specialty of this landscape contractor.

I. M. Landscaping
22678 Flamingo Street
Woodland Hills, CA 91364
(818) 703–6334
Landscape contractor who selects, installs, and maintains plant materials with great care.

Russell Palmer
Masonry Contractor
72 Glen Street
Natick, MA 01760
(617) 653–8567
Brick paving and construction of drywalls are specialties.

William Rein
Germania Masonry
2811 NE Glisan Street
Portland, OR 97232
(503) 231–7178
Particular expertise in masonry walls, patios, gates, and chimneys.

Rockwater Limited
P.O. Box 882
Amagansett, NY 11930
(516) 267–7573
Specialists in the construction of waterfalls, natural ponds, and swimming pools.

Roger Rogan
Studio 2
P.O. Box 212
Free Union, VA 22940
(804) 973–1281
Mason whose expertise includes the construction and fine detailing of stone walls, patios, columns, and entrances.

Gary Schulte
Jay Harlow
RR 1, Box 430A
High Falls, NY 12440
(914) 687–9226
Builders and craftsmen who specialize in the construction of rustic structures and furniture made of Eastern cedar.

Pam Sorrentino
South of Commons Road
Little Compton, RI 02837
(401) 635–8470
Landscape gardener with great expertise in perennials and seaside gardening.

Jack Stone—Westwood Pools Co.
3246 Barrington Avenue
Los Angeles, CA 90066
(213) 397–4020
Contractor who excels in the installation of pools, spas, and fountains as well as stonework, paving, and tile.

Ronald Vandehey
10666 S.W. Maopa Street
Portland, OR 97219
(503) 222–2366
Landscape contractor who excels in the placement of large stones and construction of dry stone walls.

Robert Zani
Homestead Tree & Landscaping Co.
19 Homestead Street
Lexington, MA 02173
(617) 862–4537
Landscape contractor particularly adept at placement of large stones in hard-to-reach garden areas.

Architectural Antiques and Garden Ornaments

Architectural antiques and ornaments add a personal touch to a garden. The following list includes sources for ornaments featured in this book as well as others recommended by garden designers.

British-American Marketing Services Ltd.
251 Welsh Pool Road
Lionville, PA 19353
(215) 363–0400
Fine selection of fiberglass reproductions of eighteenth-century garden ornaments.

Florentine Craftsmen Inc.
46–24 28th Street
Long Island City, NY 11101
(718) 937–7632
Ornamental sculpture, fountains, and furnishings including lead planters, urns, and statuary; wrought iron and cast aluminum furniture; birdbaths, sundials, and stone planters. Catalogue available.

The Garden Concepts Collection
P.O. Box 214233
Memphis, TN 38124
(901) 682–1109
Well-proportioned garden ornaments including gazebos, gates, statuary, planters, wood benches, Victorian birdhouses, arbors, and arches. Catalogue available.

Great American Salvage Company
Main Offices:
3 Main Street
Montpelier, VT 05602
(802) 223–7711

34 Cooper Square
New York, NY 10003
(212) 505–0070
Restored architectural antiques including cornices, ironwork, columns, gates, fountains, garden structures, and gargoyles. Six showrooms on East Coast.

Haddonstone Ltd.
Seahorse Trading Company, Inc. (Importers)
P.O. Box 677
Berryville, VA 22611
(703) 955–1677
Decorative and functional stoneware including urns, planters, and balustrades. Catalogue available.

Marge Hammond
1155 N.W. 35th Street
Corvallis, OR 97219
(503) 752–7306
Sculptor who specializes in cast stone with handcarved detailing including garden sculpture, benches, and fountains.

International Terra Cotta, Inc.
690 N. Robertson Boulevard
Los Angeles, CA 90069–1051
(213) 657–3752

Atlanta Decorative Arts Center/320
351 Peachtree Hills Avenue, N.E.
Atlanta, GA 30305–4572
(404) 261–4061

Turtle Creek Business Center/109
1931 Market Center Boulevard
Dallas, TX 75207–3316
(214) 744–1269
Extensive selection of terra cotta in a wide variety of architectural styles. Sandstone statuary, fountains, urns, vases, and architectural details. Will custom fabricate to specifications. Many styles also available in fiberglass. Catalogue available.

Irreplaceable Artifacts
14 Second Avenue
New York, NY 10003
(212) 777–2900
Antique ornaments from demolished buildings.

Lazy Hill Farm Designs
Lazy Hill Road
Colerain, NC 27924
(919) 356–2828 / 356–2838
Birdhouses reminiscent of English dovecotes hand-crafted from cypress with cedar shingles.

Kenneth Lynch & Sons, Inc.
Box 488
Wilton, CT 06897
(203) 762–8363
One of the world's largest dealers in garden statuary. Their extensive catalogues feature stone, bronze, and wrought iron garden ornaments including statuary, planters, finials, birdbaths, fountains, sundials, and gazebos.

Minsterstone Ltd.
Ascot Designs (Importers)
286 Congress Street
Boston, MA 02210
(617) 451–9173
Handcrafted furniture, containers, sculpture, and garden ornaments, in a wide variety of styles, made from Minsterstone, a reconstructed stone. Catalogue available.

Provender
Tiverton Four Corners
3883 Main Road
Tiverton, RI 02878
(401) 624–8096
Garden ornaments, terra cotta pots, baskets, and books.

Robinson Iron
P.O. Box 1119
Robinson Road
Alexander City, AL 35010
(205) 329–8486
Classic cast iron garden ornaments and furniture including fountains, birdbaths and birdhouses, statuary, urns, vases, and hitching posts as well as lighting fixtures in a wide range of styles and finishes.

Michael Schmitt
923 Saint Vincent Street
Santa Barbara, CA 93101
(805) 965–9752
Metal sculptor specializing in such garden structures as arbors, lights, supports for trees, and awnings. Will fabricate to specifications.

The Stone Works
8627 Melrose Avenue
Los Angeles, CA 90069
(213) 659–8614
Antique and reproduction garden ornaments in stone, including urns, amphoras, Peruvian pots, volcanic planters, olive oil jars, fossil stone, and table bases.

Urban Archaeology
137 Spring Street
New York, NY 10012
(212) 431–6969
Unique antique garden ornaments including statuary, planters, urns, fences, and fountains; new cast iron items from Robinson Iron.

Wind & Weather
P.O. Box 2320
Mendocino, CA 95460
(707) 937–0323
Catalogue of weather instruments, weathervanes, and sundials.

Zona
97 Greene Street
New York, NY 10012
(212) 925–6750
Diverse and always changing selection of garden furniture and ornaments including terra cotta pots, English garden tools, and windbells by Paolo Soleri.

Outdoor Furniture

Wholesale and retail manufacturers as well as craftspeople, mail-order suppliers, and specialty stores, all of whom offer outdoor furniture featured in this book.

Bergdorf Goodman
754 Fifth Avenue
New York, NY 10019
(212) 753–7300
Fine selection of antique garden furniture.

British-American Marketing Services Ltd.
251 Welsh Pool Road
Lionville, PA 19353
(215) 363–0400
Importer and manufacturer of classic, solid-teak furniture with traditional mortise and tenon joinery. Many designs dating from the early 1800s. Catalogue available.

Brown Jordan
P.O. Box 5688
El Monte, CA 91734
(818) 443–8971
Elegant yet durable aluminum furniture with Ultra-Fuse finish and Alumicane, vinyl-strap, or mesh seating. Catalogue available. Contact them for a list of dealers in your area.

Johns H. Congdon Furniture
R.F.D. #1
Moretown, VT 05660
(802) 496–4767
Custom, handcarved wood furniture.

Country Casual
17317 Germantown Road
Germantown, MD 20874–2999
(301) 540–0040
Designer and importer of solid-teak furniture, planters, and swings. Catalogue available.

Grant's
One Wilmington Road
Lake Placid, NY 12946
(518) 523–3400
Rustic garden benches in birch and cedar reminiscent of turn-of-the-century Adirondack camp furniture. Each piece is handcrafted and unique. Catalogue available.

Grosfillex
Muhlenberg Industrial Mall
4201 Pottsville Pike
Reading, PA 19605
(215) 921–9151

319 Lambert Street
Oxnard, CA 93030
(805) 983–8075
Synthetic-resin furniture and umbrellas. Cushions and umbrellas of Dralon. Catalogue available. Contact them for a list of dealers in your area.

Horticultural Design Products
Lenora Square, Suite 201
1000 Lenora Street
Seattle, WA 98121
(206) 292–8155
Furniture, Italian stone containers, terra cotta pots, ornaments.

Lister Teak, Inc.
561 Exton Commons
Exton, PA 19341
(800) 345–TEAK
Classic English garden furniture.

Lloyd-Flanders
3010 Tenth Street
P.O. Box 500
Menominee, MI 49858
(800) 526–9894
Durable, all-weather wicker furniture in traditional as well as contemporary styles. Aluminum frames with baked-on-enamel finish.

Lyon-Shaw
P.O. Box 2069
Salisbury, NC 28145
(704) 636–8270
Wrought iron furniture in classic as well as contemporary styles. Catalogue available. Mainly to the trade; contact them for a list of dealers in your area.

The McGuire Company
1201 Bryant Street
San Francisco, CA 94103
(415) 626–1414
Fine solid-teak, wicker, rattan, black bamboo, willow, and redwood furniture inspired by historical designs for indoor as well as outdoor use. Primarily to the trade; write for information or ask your decorator or landscape architect for their catalogue.

Pembroke Collection
Simms & Thayer
205 Oak Street
Pembroke, MA 02359
(617) 826–7221
Reproductions of early estate furniture. Catalogue available.

Pompeii Fine Casual Furniture
255 N.W. 25th Street
Miami, FL 33127
(305) 576–2339
Rust-proof aluminum furniture in a wide variety of styles. Custom sizes and finishes available. Mainly to the trade; contact them for a list of dealers in your area.

Santa Barbara Designs
P.O. Box 90610
Santa Barbara, CA 93190
(805) 965–3071
Handcrafted canvas umbrellas in teak, alder, mahogany, and oak with brass hardware; canvas umbrella covers. Handcrafted outdoor furniture in teak and solid cast bronze. Catalogue available.

Summit Furniture Inc.
Customer Service Desk
783 Redwood Avenue
Sand City, CA 93955
(408) 394–4401

Luten Clarey Stern, Inc.
1059 Third Avenue
New York, NY 10021
(212) 838–6420
First Cabin and Aperture handcrafted natural teak furniture. Catalogue available.

Triconfort
Allibert, Inc.
1200 Highway 27 South
P.O. Box 1200
Stanley, NC 28164
(704) 263–9155
White, lacquered, synthetic expanded-resin furniture with Resiceram coating; machine-washable cushions of Dralon. Rectangular and round umbrellas with placemats and coasters to match. Catalogue available. Mainly to the trade; contact them for a list of dealers in your area.

Tropitone Furniture Co.
P.O. Box 3197
Sarasota, FL 33578
(813) 355–2715
Durable all-aluminum, powder-coated furniture with vinyl lacing. Washable, outdoor-tested cushions made of Eva-Dri foam. Vinyl-coated, polyester-fiber fabric coverings in a wide range of patterns and colors. Catalogue available. Mainly to the trade; contact them for a list of dealers in your area.

Vanderbilt & Co.
1429 Main Street
St. Helena, CA 94574
(707) 963–1010
Garden containers and furniture.

Weatherend Estate Furniture
Imagineering Inc.
P.O. Box 648
Rockland, ME 04841–9990
(207) 596–6483
Furniture of natural or painted mahogany as well as teak, designed after the classic, summer "cottage" style, outdoor furniture popular at the turn of the century. Catalogue available.

The Wicker Works
267 Eighth Street
San Francisco, CA 94103
(415) 626–6730
Wicker, handcarved wood, and rattan furniture. Catalogue available. Mainly to the trade; contact them for dealers in your area.

Stephen Zimmer Furniture
West Main Road
Little Compton, RI 02837
(401) 635–2838
Handcrafted Bermuda benches, tables, and chairs.

Garden Supplies

The following list includes garden suppliers with extensive mail-order catalogues.

Burpee Essentials of Good Gardening
Warminster, PA 18974
(800) 327–3049
Catalogue of garden accessories, including quality tools, garden furniture, flower-arrangement supplies, books, and many accessories made especially for children.

Gardener's Eden
P.O. Box 737
San Francisco, CA 94120–7307
(415) 428–9292
Catalogue features garden accents and furniture, many of which are unique; garden tools, planters, vases, and flower-arrangement supplies as well as books are included.

Gardener's Supply
128 Intervale Road
Burlington, VT 05401
(802) 863–1700
Catalogue of tools and equipment for the gardener from seed starting to planting, weeding, watering, fertilizing, mulching, and organic pest controls.

Smith & Hawken
25 Corte Madera
Mill Valley, CA 94941
(415) 383–4050 (for credit card orders)

Mill Valley Store
(415) 381–0279

Palo Alto Store
705 Stanford Center
Palo Alto, CA 94304
(415) 321–0403
Garden tools and pruning supplies, watering equipment, furniture and garden ornaments, gloves, and books. Mail-order as well as retail stores in Mill Valley and Palo Alto.

Lighting

Following is a list of manufacturers of lighting fixtures. Contact them for dealers in your area.

BEGA/FS
Forms + Surfaces
Box 50442
Santa Barbara, CA 93150
(805) 565–1575
European outdoor luminaires in cast aluminum and stainless steel for all lighting situations. Sleek, contemporary lines. Catalogue available.

Genie House
P.O. Box 456
Charles Street
Medford, NJ 08055
(609) 654–6666
Handsome, handcrafted lighting fixtures with traditional styling, including lanterns for lamp posts or garden lighting in antique brass, antique copper, or verdigris. Catalogue available.

Greenlee Landscape Lighting
1220 Champion Circle, Suite 116
Carrollton, TX 75006
(214) 484–0787
Durable wall washers, grade-mounted and tree-mounted uplights, and recessed well lights in cast aluminum or cast red brass. Catalogue available.

Kim Lighting, Inc.
16555 East Gale Avenue
City of Industry, CA 91749
(213) 968–5666
Wide selection of outdoor lighting fixtures for pathways, courtyards, walls, stairways, and planters. Catalogue available.

Nightscaping by Loran, Inc.
1705 East Colton Avenue
Redlands, CA 92373
(714) 794–2121
Elegantly designed yet durable lighting for all outdoor applications including path lighting, underwater lighting, and minilights. Catalogue available.

Retail Nurseries

Sources for plant materials listed below are mail-order only, unless otherwise stated. Catalogues are available from most, generally for a nominal charge of $1 to $2, which often may be credited against a purchase.

Abbey Garden
4620 Carpinteria Avenue
Carpinteria, CA 93013
(805) 684–5112
Wide variety of fascinating cacti in 1-inch to 4-inch pots. Write for their fine catalogue.

The Antique Rose Emporium
Route 5, Box 143
Brenham, TX 77833
(409) 836–9051
Old garden roses and perennials. Visitors welcomed to their cottage garden and perennial display garden. Write for their extensive, very informative catalogue.

Appalachian Wildflower Nursery
Route 1, Box 275A
Reedsville, PA 17084
(717) 667–6998
Wildflowers and rare plants. Visit the nursery or write for their catalogue.

Armstrong Roses
P.O. Box 1020
Somis, CA 93066
(800) 338–7428
Roses for all purposes including groundcovers. Color catalogue available.

The Bayberry
Montauk Highway
Amagansett, NY 11930
(516) 267–3000
Landscape design, plant material, and garden furniture and accessories. Visitors welcome to wander through extensive display gardens featuring perennials, ornamental grasses, and specimen trees.

Bigelow Nurseries
455 West Main Street
P.O. Box 718
Northboro, MA 01532
(617) 845–2143
More than 400 acres of nursery stock including shrubs, trees, and perennials. Call for garden center hours.

Kurt Bluemel, Inc.
2740 Greene Lane
Baldwin, MD 21013
(301) 557–7229
Ornamental grasses, rushes, sedges, perennials, bamboos, and ferns. Write for their catalogue.

Caprilands Herb Farm
534 Silver Street
Coventry, CT 06238
(203) 742–7244
Everything for the herb gardener including an extensive selection of seeds, plants, books, and ornaments such as bee skeps. Thirty-one different gardens; shops and greenhouses open year-round. Write for their catalogue.

Carlson's Gardens
Box 305
South Salem, NY 10590
(914) 763–5958
Native azaleas, including many fragrant varieties, and Carlson's own late-blooming, hybrid 'Postscript' azaleas. Write for their amusing catalogue. Gardens open by appointment only.

Carroll Gardens
P.O. Box 310
444 East Main Street
Westminster, MD 21157
(301) 848–5422
Ornamental grasses, dwarf evergreens, perennials, shrubs, trees, and groundcovers. Catalogue available.

Cooley's Gardens
P.O. Box 126
Silverton, OR 97381
(503) 873–5463
Irises in every color imaginable. Write for their extensive color catalogue.

Cummins Garden
22 Robertsville Road
Marlboro, NJ 07746
(201) 536–2591
Azaleas, rhododendrons, dwarf evergreens, and perennials. Write for the catalogue; call ahead if you wish to visit the nursery.

Desert to Jungle Nursery
3211 West Beverly Boulevard
Montebello, CA 90640
(213) 722–3976
General nursery specializing in rare and exotic plants. One of the largest selections of grasses on the West Coast.

Faddegon's Nursery, Inc.
1140 Troy–Schenectady Road
Latham, NY 12110
(518) 785–6726
Garden center with greenhouses specializing in residential and interior landscaping.

Gale Nurseries
1716 School House Road
Gwynedd, PA 19436
(215) 699–4714
Full-service nursery specializing in the design and implementation of period, native, and contemporary gardens.

Gossler Farms Nursery
1200 Weaver Road
Springfield, OR 97478–9663
(503) 746–6611
Ornamental shrubs and trees including many hard-
to-find varieties of magnolias, Stewartias, and
hamamelis; small specimens only. Nursery and gardens open almost any time by appointment. Catalogue
available.

Greenlee Nursery
301 East Franklin Avenue
Pomona, CA 91766
(714) 629–9045
Ornamental grasses, rushes, and sedges. Nursery open
by appointment. Write for their informative catalogue.

Greer Gardens
1280 Goodpasture Island Road
Eugene, OR 97401
(503) 686–8266
Dwarf evergreens, Japanese maples, azaleas, and
rhododendrons. Write for the catalogue.

Allen C. Haskell
787 Shawmut Avenue
New Bedford, MA 02746
(617) 993–9047
Perennials, evergreens, groundcovers, herbs, stan-
dards.

Helderledge Farm
R.D. #2, Box 408
Altamont, NY 12009
(518) 765–4702
Herbaceous perennials and hardy plants suitable to
the local hardiness zone; landscape design and horticultural services offered.

High Country Rosarium
1717 Downing at Park Avenue
Denver, CO 80218
(303) 832–4026
Catalogue of roses hardy to the area including old
garden roses, shrub and species roses. All roses grown
on their own root. Rose collections offered include:
Hedge Collection, Bird Lovers Collection, and
Drought Tolerant Collection. Seeds also available.

Hillside Gardens
Litchfield Road
P.O. Box 614
Norfolk, CT 06058
(203) 542–5345
Hardy perennials, including many unusual vari-
eties. Gardens open by appointment or by chance.
Plant list available.

Jackson & Perkins Co.
1 Rose Lane
Medford, OR 97501
(503) 776–2400
Reputed to be the world's largest rose grower. Catalogue also includes flowering trees, fruit trees, and
berries.

Kale's Nursery
133 Carter Road
Princeton, NJ 08540
(609) 921–9248
Full-service nursery, including garden design, installation, and stonework.

Kasch's Garden Center & Nursery
2500 Southeast Tacoma Street at McLoughlin
Portland, OR 97202
(503) 231–7711
Full-service garden center with a good selection of
plant materials and garden supplies.

Keil Brothers
220–15 Horace Harding Boulevard
Bayside, NY 11364
(718) 224–2020
Full-service nursery and garden center, specializing in
heathers and heaths, rock garden plants, and dwarf
conifers.

Klehm Nursery
Route 5, 197 Penny Road
South Barrington, IL 60010
(312) 551–3715
Growers of peonies since the late 1890s; also known
for their fine selection of irises, hostas, and daylilies.
Informative, illustrated catalogue. Visitors are wel-
come at the farm in Champaign–Urbana.

Henry Leuthardt Nurseries, Inc.
Montauk Highway
Box 666
East Moriches, NY 11940
(516) 878–1387
Espaliers, dwarf and semidwarf fruit trees, berries,
table and dessert grapevines. Call for nursery hours
and price list.

Lilypons Water Gardens
6800 Lilypons Road
P.O. Box 10
Lilypons, MD 21717–0010
(301) 874–5133
or
P.O. Box 188
Brookshire, TX 77423–0188
(713) 934–8525
Hardy and tropical aquatic plants, including a
selection of night-blooming tropical lilies, lotus,
and bog plants. Informative, illustrated catalogue.
Visitors are welcome, especially for the annual
Lotus Blossom Festival.

Logee's Greenhouses
55 North Street
Danielson, CT 06239
(203) 774–8038
Extensive selection of begonias, rare plants, tropicals, herbs, and geraniums including many scented varieties. Illustrated catalogue available.

Lowe's Own Root Roses
Six Sheffield Road
Nashua, NH 03062
(603) 888–2214
Small nursery specializing in old garden roses, carefully selected from private collections in Europe and the United States; an excellent selection of ramblers and climbers is featured. Write for the plant list.

McAllister Water Gardens
7420 St. Helena Street
Yountville, CA 94599
(707) 253–1115
Garden center offering perennials, ornamental grasses, and aquatics.

Magic Growers
1300 North Altadena Drive
Pasadena, CA 91107
(818) 791–3131
Largest selection of herbaceous flowering-plant materials in southern California, including many varieties difficult to locate on the West Coast. Wholesale only; ask your landscape architect or contractor to contact them.

Meadowbrook Farm
1633 Washington Lane
Meadowbrook, PA 19046
(215) 887–5900
Extensive selection of plants for the conservatory, topiary of all forms and sizes, and over 600 varieties of perennials and ornamental grasses, shrubs, and trees. Strong emphasis on unusual and hard-to-find varieties suitable for the collector. Greenhouse and nursery open year-round.

Merry Gardens
Mechanic Street
Camden, ME 04843
(207) 236–9064
Extensive selection of herbs, fuchsias, ivies (including variegated types), and unusual miniature, dwarf and scented-leaved geraniums. Informative catalogues available. Visitors are welcome; special exhibits are planned during summer.

Milaeger's Gardens
4838 Douglas Avenue
Racine, WI 53402
(414) 639–2040
Hardy perennials and herbs, including a selection of prairie plants and grasses. Write for their "Perennial Wishbook."

Millane Nurseries and Tree Experts, Inc.
604 Main Street
Cromwell, CT 06416
(203) 635–5500
Extensive selection of specimen shade trees, pines, and shrubs, including many unusual hybrids available at the garden center.

Miller Nurseries
West Lake Road
Canandaigua, NY 14424
(800) 828–9630
Known for their hardy fruits and berries, they also carry eight roses proven hardy to −25°F. Informative catalogue includes some hardy shade trees and garden supplies as well.

Robert W. Montgomery Landscape Nursery
Box 67-C, Route 113
Chester Springs, PA 19425
(215) 363–2477
Full-service nursery with garden center and greenhouses providing a wide selection of perennials and unique plant materials, landscape supplies, and outdoor furniture.

Nor'east Miniature Roses
58 Hammond Street
Rowley, MA 01969
(617) 948–7964
Naturally dwarf roses growing 12 to 18 inches tall on average (some grow only 5 to 8 inches). Color catalogue. Display gardens open daily.

Nuccio's Nurseries
P.O. Box 6160
3555 Chaney Trail
Altadena, CA 91001
(818) 794–3383
Extensive catalogue of rare camellias and azaleas, including an impressive list of their own hybrids. Visitors are welcome.

Oliver Nurseries, Inc.
1159 Bronson Road
Fairfield, CT 06430
(203) 259–5609
Retail nursery specializing in rare and unusual dwarf conifers and alpine plants as well as rhododendrons and azaleas. Display gardens feature mature specimens of plants available in the catalogue. They do not ship plants, however.

Theodore Payne Foundation
10459 Tuxford Street
Sun Valley, CA 91352
(818) 768–1802
Nonprofit foundation dedicated to the preservation of California flora. Write for their extensive plant list of wildflowers and native plants, many of which are adaptable to higher elevations, or visit the nursery Tuesday through Saturday.

Pickering Nurseries, Inc.
670 Kingston Road
Pickering, Ontario L1V 1A6
Canada
(416) 839–2111
A fine selection of roses, including many antique and rare varieties. Purchases by mail only. Write for their beautifully illustrated catalogue.

Rice Creek Gardens
1315 66th Avenue, N.E.
Minneapolis, MN 55432
(612) 574–1197
Extensive catalogue of perennials, alpines for the sun or shade garden, wildflowers, ferns, and interesting selections of unusual flowering shrubs, dwarf and weeping conifers. Usually open six days a week.

Rock Knoll Nursery
9210 U.S. 50
Hillsboro, OH 45133–8546
(513) 393–1278
Catalogue of over 400 varieties of unusual rock plants, shade plants, perennials, and dwarf evergreens.

Roses by Fred Edmunds
6235 S.W. Kahle Road
Wilsonville, OR 97070
(503) 638–4671
Primarily modern, hybrid tea roses, including many of their own patent. A mail-order nursery, it does not have display gardens; travelers are welcome to visit their fields from mid-September while the blooms last, however. Illustrated catalogue.

Roses of Yesterday and Today, Inc.
802 Brown's Valley Road
Watsonville, CA 95076
(408) 724–3537
Old, rare, unusual, and selected modern roses from all over the world. Informative catalogue includes personal and historical notes. The display gardens are in fullest bloom from mid-May to mid-June.

San Marcos Growers
125 South San Marcos Road
Santa Barbara, CA 93111
(805) 683–1561
General nursery offering a number of unusual native plants.

San Simeon Nursery
HCR-33 Villa Creek Road
Cayucos, CA 93430
(805) 995–2466
Growers of cacti and succulents—many unusual and hard to find—as well as drought-tolerant plants native to California and Australia.

Sandy Mush Herb Nursery
Route 2, Surrett Cove Road
Leicester, NC 28748
(704) 683–2014
Rare herbs, fragrant foliage plants, and perennials, including culinary and medicinal varieties; bee, tea and dye plants; groundcovers, potpourris, and bonsai. Handbook includes plant list, growing guide, and recipes.

Santa Barbara Water Gardens & Landscapes
P.O. Box 4353
Santa Barbara, CA 93140
(805) 969–5129 or 969–5302
Extensive selection of specimen, hardy, and tropical aquatic plants. Staff experienced in water-garden design, construction, and maintenance. Call for plant list and nursery hours.

Shelter Island Nurseries
St. Mary's Road
Shelter Island, NY 11964
(516) 749–0490
The garden center, which specializes in seashore plants, is affiliated with the Baier Lustgarden Farms and Nurseries.

Singers' Growing Things
17806 Plummer Street
Northridge, CA 91325
(818) 993–1903
Primarily a mail-order nursery specializing in succulents other than cacti. Greenhouses and garden open to visitors Thursday through Saturday or by appointment.

Siskiyou Rare Plant Nursery
2825 Cummings Road
Medford, OR 97501
(503) 772–6846
Alpine and rare dwarf plants for the woodland and rock gardens. Many of the more unusual varieties are a real challenge, even for the experienced gardener! A source for the true connoisseur. Write for their catalogue.

Smith & Hawken
25 Corte Madera
Mill Valley, CA 94941
(415) 381–0279
(415) 383–4050 (credit card orders)
Full-scale nursery selling natives and perennials. Extensive catalogue.

J. Franklin Styer Nurseries
Route 1
Concordville, PA 19331
(215) 459–2400
Provides all services, from design to installation and maintenance. Full selection of plant and landscape materials as well as unique garden ornaments.

Sunnyslope Gardens
8638 Huntington Drive
San Gabriel, CA 91775
(818) 287–4071
Extensive selection of chrysanthemums, including
their own introductions, Saga, Ise, and many prize-
winning varieties. Write for their catalogue.

Swan Island Dahlias
P.O. Box 800
Canby, OR 97013
(503) 266–7711
Growers of fine dahlias for over fifty years. Extensive
color catalogue. Farm open daily. Annual Dahlia
Festival in September.

Tree of Life Nursery
P.O. Box 736
San Juan Capistrano, CA 92693
(805) 481–5996
Nursery specializing in plant materials native to
California. Wholesale only. Send for their catalogue.

Tripple Brook Farm
37 Middle Road
Southampton, MA 01073
(413) 527–4626
Interesting, small catalogue includes many bamboos
and ornamental grasses hardy to the area; trees and
shrubs including pomegranates, guava, and carob;
vines such as kiwi, passionflower, and porcelain vine.

Turk Hessellund Nursery
1255 Coast Village Road
Santa Barbara, CA 93108
(805) 969–5871
General nursery that offers an especially good selection
of rare and exotic plants.

Van Ness Water Gardens
2460 North Euclid Avenue
Upland, CA 91786
(714) 982–2425
Color catalogue includes hardy and tropical water
lilies, bog plants, grasses, and everything necessary to
build and maintain a water garden. Gardens open
Tuesday through Saturday.

Andre Viette Farm & Nursery
Route 1, Box 16
Fishersville, VA 22939
(703) 943–2315
Growers of rare and unusual perennials, especially
flowering varieties, rock garden perennials, woodland
plants, and daylilies. Write for the catalogue.

Waterloo Gardens
200 North Whitford Road
Exton, PA 19341
(215) 363–0800
or
136 Lancaster Avenue
Devon, PA 19333
(215) 293–0800
Full-service nursery offering a wide variety of perennials, roses, topiary, rare conifers, azaleas, and
rhododendrons; garden pools, fountains, and outdoor
furniture. Open daily.

Wayside Gardens
Hodges, SC 29695–0001
(800) 845–1124
Color catalogue includes a vast selection of perennials,
shrubs, and trees, including many rare and unusual
hybrids.

Western Hills Nursery
16250 Coleman Valley Road
Occidental, CA 95465
(707) 874–8731
All-round nursery that also offers rare and exotic
plants.

Weston Nurseries
Route 135
Hopkinton, MA 01748–0186
(617) 435–3414
General nursery offering a wide selection of plant
materials, including many perennials, old-fashioned
shrubs, and large-caliper trees.

White Flower Farm
Route 63
Litchfield, CT 06759–0050
Mail Order: (203) 496–1661
Retail Store: (203) 567–8789
Informative, illustrated garden book offers perennials
hardy to the area, including forsythia hardy to
−30°F; daylilies, hostas, ferns, and fine garden
tools. Store and gardens open mid-April through
October.

Seeds

Applewood Seed Co.
5380 Vivian Street
Arvada, CO 80002
(303) 431–6283
Wildflower-seed catalogue.

W. Atlee Burpee Co.
300 Park Avenue
Warminster, PA 18991
(215) 674–4915
Extensive catalogue of flowers, vegetable, and fruit seeds, including special collections of seeds and plants with detailed garden plans by Alice Recknagel Ireys.

Environmental Seed Producers
P.O. Box 5904
El Monte, CA 91734
(818) 442–3330
Wildflower-seed catalogue.

Johnny's Selected Seeds
Foss Hill Road
Albion, ME 04910
(207) 437–9294
Catalogue includes seeds for flowers, herbs, and unusual vegetables, all selected for their flavor and hardiness.

Park Seed Co.
Cokesbury Road
Greenwood, SC 29647–0001
(800) 845–3369
Catalogue of seeds for flowers and vegetables as well as a selection of perennial plants.

Putney Nursery, Inc.
Box 51
Putney, VT 05346
(802) 387–5577
Seeds for flowers that attract bees, for culinary and aromatic herbs, and for wildflowers, including a wildflower mix specially formulated for the New England environment. Plants also available. Write for the catalogue or visit the nursery.

The Rosemary House, Inc.
120 South Market Street
Mechanicsburg, PA 17055
(717) 766–6581
Extensive selection of herb seeds. Herb list available, or visit and enjoy the eighteenth-century herb garden.

Shepherd's Garden Seeds
7389 West Zayante Road
Felton, CA 95018
(408) 335–5311
or
30 Irene Street
Torrington, CT 06790
(203) 482–3638
Catalogue includes European vegetable seeds as well as seeds for edible flowers, everlastings, and herbs.

Thompson & Morgan
P.O. Box 1308
Jackson, NJ 08527
(800) 367–7333
Substantial catalogue includes thousands of seeds, ranging from annuals and perennials to vegetables, herbs, tropical, and subtropical plants to trees and shrubs.

Vermont Bean Seed Company
Garden Lane
Fair Haven, VT 05743
(802) 265–3082
Informative catalogue of annual and perennial flowers, herbs, and vegetables. Organic growing, season extension, and companion planting for insect control are featured. Special seed collections include a Child's Garden and Shade Garden.

Vermont Wildflower Farm
Route 7
Charlotte, VT 05445
(802) 425–3500
Catalogue of wildflower seeds specially grown for each region of the United States as well as all-perennial and all-annual mixes. Wildflower gardens and gift shop open daily May through mid-October.

Bulbs

Jan de Graaff Oregon Bulb Farms
14071 N.E. Arndt Road
Aurora, OR 97002
(503) 226–7425
Exquisite catalogue of lily bulbs, including Oriental, Aurelian ("Trumpet" lilies), Asiatic and Short Asiatic hybrids.

McLure & Zimmerman
1422 West Thorndale
Chicago, IL 60660
(312) 274–0113
Extensive catalogue.

John Scheepers, Inc.
R.D. 6, Phillipsburg Road
Middletown, NY 10940
(914) 342–3727
Flower specialists with spring and fall catalogues of bulbs from around the world.

Mary Mattison van Schaik
R.F.D. Box 181
Cavendish, VT 05142
(802) 226–7338
Catalogue of imported Dutch bulbs.

Every effort was made to ensure the accuracy of the information in this listing. With time, however, addresses and names do change, so a compilation of this sort cannot be absolutely precise, despite all efforts.

Design

J.C. SUARÈS
JOSEPH RUTT

The photographs were shot with Rolleiflex cameras
on Ektachrome and Fujichrome color reversal film.
Principal processing by Duggal Color Projects, New York, New York.
Pacific Northwest sequence processed by A & I Color Laboratories, Los Angeles, California.

The text was composed in Garamond Old Style by Trufont Typographers, Inc.,
Hicksville, New York.

The book was printed and bound by
Toppan Printing Company, Ltd.,
Tokyo, Japan.